BECOMING
A
CFI

A story about the right seat.

RADEK WYRZYKOWSKI

Order this book online at www.trafford.com
or email orders@trafford.com

Most Trafford titles are also available at major online book retailers.

Print information available on the last page.

ISBN: 978-1-6987-0691-7 (sc)
ISBN: 978-1-6987-0690-0 (hc)
ISBN: 978-1-6987-0689-4 (e)

Library of Congress Control Number: 2021907594

Trafford rev. 04/15/2021

www.trafford.com
North America & international
toll-free: 844-688-6899 (USA & Canada)
fax: 812 355 4082

CONTENTS

"When Radek Wyrzykowski asked me if I might be interested in reviewing his book *Becoming a CFI: A Story about the Right Seat*, my first instinct was caution: who am I to review a book about flying? I am not a pilot, and my flying experience is limited to being a passenger on commercial flights. My curiosity was raised because I am a Coast Guard sailing captain with 50 years of experience, and the physics of flying and sailing are similar. I am glad I read the book. It is riveting for both fliers and nonfliers. It reads so well that I went through it in three hours and could not put it down. The second part of the title, *A Story about the Right Seat*, provides the real sense of the book. Clearly, the author is a highly experienced and accomplished GA pilot and CFI. But there is much more than that. His own experiences are told with a poetic flare, mixing CFI professionalism with deep romanticism of flying and with humanism of a caring instructor. Radek's eagerness to share his experience and advice with the reader jumps out from every page. The book blends humble stories of Radek's own flying lessons with his advanced methods of teaching others. The small book packs a lot of hard CFI knowledge combined with psychology, and yet it reads like an adventure book. As a sailor, I could appreciate his lessons on radio comms, weather, the methodical preparations needed for a safe flight, and dealing with inexperienced crew.

The book is understandable by everyone but valuable even to experienced CFIs. Its thoughtful and robust insights are the perfect prescription for anyone with a serious ambition to be a great CFI. Masterful."

Bohdan W. Oppenheim, PhD
Professor and Director, Healthcare Systems
Engineering Program, LMU
US Coast Guard Captain's License

"(...) we can make rules to require certain professional behavior, but professionalism is a lot more than rule-driven behaviors. It's a mindset. It's an attitude that drives you to do the right thing—every time, all the time."

Randy Babbitt
Former FAA Administrator

FOREWORD

A great American motivational writer William Arthur Ward (December 17, 1921–March 30, 1994) once said that the mediocre teacher tells, the good teacher explains, the superior teacher demonstrates but the great teacher inspires.

This gem of a book is about inspiring people to achieve a unique dream—becoming a pilot. Combining great allure and great responsibility, learning to fly an airplane is for the select few.

Much has been written about teaching the technical aspect of aviation but very little about inspiring students through the challenges of learning a skill that few possess.

Radek Wyrzykowski has inspired hundreds of students to become private pilots, instrument-rated pilots, commercial pilots, and CFIs over a twenty-year teaching career. His book contains dozens of useful, practical tips that will help you help your students to keep their heads and hearts in the game.

Steve Sullivan
Cofounder and Chairman of IMC Club
CFII and student of Radek

I Fell in Love When I Was Six

Author at age six (1966)

I fell in love when I was six—the type of love that lasted me a lifetime. As a little boy, I witnessed my father getting on an airplane to travel from Rzeszow, our hometown, to Poland's capital, Warsaw, for work. It was then when I saw this beauty for the first time—a silver twin tail wheel DC-2 with square windows and a black registration number on the side of the fuselage. It was parked on the ramp, getting ready to taxi. There were no fences, no guards, and no security forces. I was able to touch it, feel it, smell the distinct odor of aviation fuel, and walk inside to see pilots going over their checklists. From that point on, I knew I had to be a pilot. Two pieces of wood nailed together in the form of an airplane accompanied my dreams for years in my childhood—dreams that I was able to realize in my late thirties.

My first airplane

Coming from the country with a tradition of aviation going back to 1920, the country about which Lynne Olson and Stanley Cloud in their book *A Question of Honor* wrote that it produced the best pilots in the world, I always had great respect for flying. General aviation was always for me a "sacred society," a brotherhood of people joined in one passion and one love—the ultimate freedom of human beings, flight. My favorite book by Janusz Meissner, *Memoirs of a Pilot*, which I had read at least ten times up to this point in my life, also supported my beliefs.

In a strange twist of faith, during the most critical crisis in my life, I was left alone by so-called friends and people who should be there for me. I was left alone when I needed them most, left alone with my thoughts and feelings, and yet every time, my only faithful friend and my childhood love was there for me to bring me back to life. In those critical moments, I was freeing myself from life by flying alone. Just me and the ultimate freedom of mankind would bring a different perspective in my life and let me know that dreams do come true.

Now I have achieved what I always wanted. I am a flight instructor. I believe that the flight instructor certificate is the highest privilege among the brotherhood of pilots. We have to prove that we are trustworthy and skilled to provide others with our experience and talent. With the benefit of a flight instructor's license comes an obligation and responsibility to be the best among the best, to train ourselves continuously and fine-tune our skills, to educate ourselves about new techniques and technologies, and to keep our flying to a higher measure. Maybe we don't realize it, but general aviation and the dream of so many of us are in great danger. One of the reasons is an inflow of flight instructors who do not care.

I want this book to be my declaration of "war," war against flight instructors with no ambition, motivation, and personality. Those who wait in line to be hired by a major airline. Those who do not care about students. Those who turn the highest privilege of our "sacred society" and my childhood dream into a "Burger King" of aviation. This is my war against mediocre, against trainers who do their jobs to a minimum, against those who do not challenge their students and themselves.

This book is not intended as a manual or a textbook. I will blend in my personal flying experience based on real-life events with my flight instructor's experience and my beliefs and philosophy on how I think it should be done.

I dedicate this book to the people who made a difference in my life. To my parents, Barbara and Roman, who raised me and believed in my dreams and taught me to stand up and go forward smiling no matter what. They passed away at age ninety-six and seventy-seven respectively.

I dedicate this book to my wife, who allowed me to dream and free feelings I had not dreamed about before. Thank you!

I dedicate this book to all the others who helped me be who I am. You know who you are! Thank you!

I also dedicate this book to my dear friend, my mentor, my flight instructor, Doug Stewart, whose wisdom and passion for flying made me a better and dedicated pilot. He once said, "Flying gives us a perspective of the world. We realize our insignificance from a cosmic viewpoint, yet at the same time, flying empowers us with the ability to have control over our destiny. What a wonderful paradox! As above so below."

CHAPTER

1

I Am A Licensed Student Pilot

Columbia County Airport (1B1) is a county-owned, public-use airport located 4 miles northeast of Hudson, New York. It is a small not-towered general aviation airport in the Hudson Valley. If you look to the west, you will see the Catskill Mountains magnificently standing in the distance, rich in wildlife, hiking trails, and ski resorts.

Despite its 100-foot-wide and over 4,000-foot-long runway 3-21, there are no commercial passenger operations out of here and the general aviation traffic is sparse. It is surrounded by open fields between small groups of trees and borders two single-lane highways to its south and west. A little old building is housing the FBO (fixed base operator) and an aviation flight school, neighboring a blue hangar made of corrugated metal sheets.

It is early November. Although most of the trees already lost their colors, it is still relatively warm. The air does not smell like an impending winter yet. But the splendor of summer is long gone.

I have been here many times before. Here, I did my first intro flight, which I received from my wife as a birthday gift a year ago. Now we visit one-bravo-one regularly with my flight instructor Doug to practice my takeoffs and landings.

I am based out of Great Barrington, Massachusetts, just 15 miles southeast of here. But that extra almost 2,000 feet of runway makes it a much better location for my struggles to land. I have twenty-two hours total in my logbook in between three different flight schools. But only ten with this one. I hope this flight school will work out for me, unlike the previous two, wherein both my flight instructors left for an airline job shortly after we started our training.

I am flying with Doug. He is shorter than me, always dressed in a vest with the logo indicating his membership with NAFI (National Association of Flight Instructors). Doug has some gray hair and an incredibly positive and happy demeanor. I can't recall a single flight during which we wouldn't laugh or he wouldn't say something funny about my flying that would always make me chuckle. General aviation is about having fun, he says every time he has a chance.

But I can't have too much fun now. I have a "dangerous" job of landing this "beast" of a Piper PA-28 Cherokee on the 4,000-foot runway in front of me. But I do feel I am up to the task today.

We are approaching the airport from the east. On the CTAF, which I have been monitoring for some time now, I hear another traffic landing on runway 3. My previous check of AWOS also indicated that the wind is calm. So runway 3 it is going to be. I gently reduce power to start my descent to the traffic pattern altitude of 1,200 feet. My eyes are outside of the cockpit, trying to see where the airport is. I want to work the radio myself, so I announce our positions and intentions using pre-memorized formulas I found in one of the textbooks about aviation communication. But where is that "invisible" airport?

I look at the directional gyro once again, trying to picture my entry to the downwind of runway 3. I should remember that the runway number on that instrument is the opposite of where the runway's approach is, but my brain is playing tricks on me. A sudden confusion is invading my brain. As I concentrate on my directional gyro, I don't see that my altitude is way too low.

"Radek decided to land off the field today," I hear the cheerful voice of my flight instructor in my headset.

A quick look at my altimeter shows us below 1,000 feet. I look again at my directional gyro, then I notice that my airspeed is on the low side. *Why are there so many gauges in this old Cherokee?* I think.

"The airport is outside, not in the cockpit," I hear Doug having fun and adding something about instrument flying. But I have no time for fun. My eyes are back outside. I have been here so many times. Why can't I see that airport every time?

But there it is. Nobody took it away. After flying slightly to the south, we enter the left traffic pattern. *Now I am home,* I think. Power reduction, flap deployment, turn to base, and final. The main gear is gently touching down the asphalt.

"Let's make it full stop!" I hear Doug's voice.

I am turning left into one of the taxiways and stop to perform the post-landing checklist. I am proud of my landing like a child whose letters are finally written how the teacher does it. As I am just about to start taxiing to the ramp, I hear my instructor's voice.

"You don't need me here anymore. Let me out. Just don't forget to come back." I see his smiling face as he opens the door and gets out of the cockpit.

For a second, shock mixes with disbelief, happiness, and concern. Then tasks at hand take over. I taxi back to the departure end of runway 3. I look again to my right to discover that for sure nobody is sitting there. I double-and triple-check all items on my pre-takeoff checklist just to be sure. I make sure that nobody is approaching for landing on the final.

"Columbia County traffic, Cherokee departing runway 3. Close traffic." Even my voice on the radio sounds different to me now.

I roll onto the runway and add full power. The airplane accelerates forward much faster than I have anticipated. In no time, I am at my rotation speed and the ground escapes below. Once again, roads become small ribbons and people disappear from view. I check to make sure the airspeed is good, and it is. I listen carefully to the sound of the engine. It does sound different. I can't put my finger on what the difference is. I check RMP, and it is where it is supposed to be. Could it be my imagination?

Now I am at the traffic pattern altitude of 1,200 feet. I should have started my turn to the crosswind leg 300 feet below. I have missed it. I promptly reduce power and level off. Now I am slightly too high.

The airport is now far behind me. I don't want to get lost. I turn to the left for the crosswind leg and reduce power to get down to my proper altitude. I see the airport in the distance to my left. *OK, it is still there,* I think to myself. I see County Route 9H below. It is my landmark for the downwind turn. With a steep left bank, I grab that road "under my left arm." Now the runway is to my left. It feels so good. I look once again to the right to make sure it is not my dream. Still, nobody there.

Abeam the approach end of the runway, I reduce power to 1,500 rpm and deploy all my flaps. It is a technique that is required by this flight school for the short runway of the Great Barrington Airport. But the only thing I know is the way the flight school wants us to land. The airplane seems to be so happy in the air that it does not want to sink as it usually does. Route 66, almost perpendicular to my flight path, is closing in on me without any mercy. Just behind it, I should be turning into the base leg. I reduce power further without looking at the rpm gauge. Now the airplane, as if aware of my struggles, kindly starts going down.

I am turning into the base leg a little farther from the runway than usual. But I am still high. The turn to final comes in what seems to be just a few seconds. I am so high that I have to reduce power to idle. But my glide path now looks perfect. The runway is closing in on me like an old friend who misses me a lot. I bring the nose of the airplane up just above the runway, and I start sinking slowly. It seems to last an eternity. The aircraft decided to take as much runway as is available to it but finally meets the ground as intended. I brake a little harder than I should. It is going to be a stop-and-go landing.

After turning the carburetor heat off, I advance the throttle to full power again. The aircraft starts rolling. But this time, it is moving much slower than I would expect. Before I can limp myself to the rotation speed, I am already in the air. I can't figure out what is happening. The airplane's nose wants to pitch up rapidly against my intense forward pressure on the yoke. I look around the cockpit, and suddenly, it hits me. I have never retracted the flaps. I reach down to the handle between the seats and slowly take out two notches. Now the Cherokee decides to sink, but my quick nose-forward action revives its speed to where it should be.

I have no time now to analyze what had just happened, but I will remember it for the rest of my life. The turn to crosswind comes quickly, and I do it at the proper altitude. On downwind, I even have time to look at the majesty of the Catskill Mountains rising on the west side of the Hudson River's gray ribbon.

The next two landings come without a glitch. "I am a licensed student pilot!" I want to shout to the entire world as I am taxiing back to pick up Doug for our return trip.

CHAPTER

2

Lost in November

It is late November, and the air is cool and dense. The temperature is not going over forty-five degrees for a few days now, but the sun is in its full glory. Only individual cumulus clouds like giant ice cream portions are floating in the distance on the horizon. The light breeze brings with it the smell of winter. Next month, snow will start covering the ground around here with its white blanket and Christmas decorations will start showing up in the neighborhood. For now, it feels like an invisible climate border. It feels like a border between fall and winter, which will be showing up here in the not-so-distant future.

I take a few hours off work and head to the airport. The Cherokee I fly is available. I know because I called in advance to make sure. Nobody flies anyway in the middle of the day. The airport is only a short twenty-minute drive from where I work, and it is perfect weather to be in the air.

Great Barrington Airport—still the same in 2021

Great Barrington Airport, like many small general aviation airports in the USA, has its own history. The airport is located in a valley surrounded by the Berkshire Mountains. Its only runway 11-29 runs parallel a narrow asphalt country road, Route 71. It is located only a few miles away from the town of Great Barrington with its population of just about seven thousand people. A small country back road is crossing the approach end of runway 29. There are no fences or gates. Quite often, cars stop on that road just a hundred yards away from the threshold to watch how airplanes land.

The road crossing the approach end of runway 29 at 7B2

It was initially a potato field before becoming a small family-owned airstrip in 1931. This unassuming airfield eventually grew into today's capacity, with a 2,500-foot paved runway. This airport is without a fence, and buildings and hangars are still the same, emanating its long and exciting history. Walter Koladza, a pilot whose family came from Poland (original name, Kolodziej), was a test pilot during World War II, and now he owns the airport for nearly sixty years. Walter was an instructor in the war training flight school at Berkshire School in Sheffield, Massachusetts, in 1940. He bought this hundred-acre facility in 1944, and now, in his late seventies, he is an authorized FAA examiner for Western New England. He is the one with whom I will have my initial private pilot certificate checkride when I am ready to become a pilot. For now, I am still just a student.

I take the clipboard with flight times from the office and head straight to the airplane parked on the ramp in front of the building. The keys are always in the aircraft. Everyone trusts one another in this neighborhood. If I want to rent one of the airplanes after hours, the only thing I need to do is call in the next morning with my flight time. I would cover the bill next time I am at the airport.

There is a light breeze, and the sky is blue. The wind sock is moving sluggishly, but it is indicating runway 29 for takeoff.

Preflight and start-up are going smoothly without anything unexpected. Run-up is taking place at the end of the short taxiway heading to the runway. It is the only taxiway at this airport, so I will need to taxi back on the runway to the end for departure.

My plan today is straightforward. As a student pilot, I can practice whatever I want within a 25-mile radius of the airport. Why not just "practice" the pleasure of being in the air? I have my sectional already folded on my kneeboard. The more I think about it, the more I like that idea. I look at the map. I will turn to the north until I see highway I-90. Then I will turn to the west, and I will follow that highway until I see the Taconic Parkway. I will follow the Taconic Parkway until I see the town of Philmont, and then I will turn to the east to return to Great Barrington. I drove those roads so many times, and I know this area very well. How difficult could it be? From the air, everything should be much easier to see anyway.

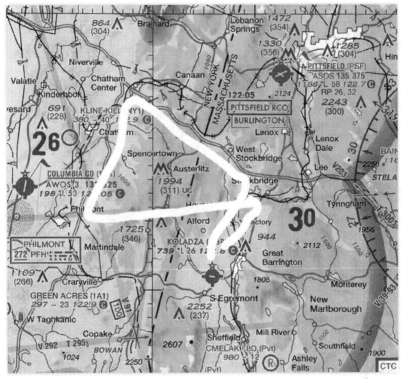

My local solo flight track

"Great Barrington traffic, Cherokee back taxiing runway two-nine for departure," my voice proudly sounds on the radio. I roll on the runway and travel to the departure end. Everything feels good. I feel like an airline pilot with thousands of hours already under my belt. Some old red Chevy truck just stopped on the road crossing the approach area to the takeoff strip. They will be watching my launch. My pride at this moment has no limits. I am a pilot!

I do a 180-degree turn at the end and position myself for takeoff. As I turn, I see a young guy with probably his girlfriend intensely watching me from behind the closed window of the parked vehicle.

"Lights, camera, switches, action," I tell myself, which means "Lights on, transponder on altitude, fuel pump on, power full forward." I make another announcement on the radio as the airplane is starting to move forward. I can feel inertia pushing me back into the seat and a little shiver from the wheels still driving on the surface. I see the airspeed needle moving clockwise. The outside world is running to the back as I approach the rotation speed. Slight back pressure on the yoke, and everything smooths out. Once again, things on the ground become smaller and smaller. Once again, I am in the air. There is something so very unique every single time about this moment. Something magical I can't explain.

I climb to 3,000 feet and make a steep bank to turn to a north-north-easterly heading. I see to my right the town of Housatonic with its paper mill and some railroad tracks. I look at the sectional, and to my euphoric happiness, I discover that I know exactly where I am. Not long after, a gray ribbon with different colors of moving little insects is crossing my flight path.

"Highway 90!" My happiness is boundless. As planned, I bank to the left to follow the highway. Now my next waypoint is the intersection with the Taconic Parkway. My eyes are bonded to the road. Time is passing by. Several roads cross the highway in many different directions, but none of them look familiar. I am flying over some large intersection, but it ends in a single-lane road when the Taconic Parkway is supposed to be a two-lane highway.

By now, it seems like hours have passed. But I look at my watch, indicating only ten minutes from when I started following I-90. Still, ten minutes should be enough, but the stubborn intersection is nowhere to be found. As I contemplate my next course of action, suddenly, a two-way highway is branching to the left of the road I now follow. Taconic! I recognize the toll plaza with its booths. Then it strikes me! There is probably a stronger wind at this altitude. Great Barrington Airport is in a valley. How could I forget about the headwind?

Now I am following another highway as planned. This time, my confidence is high. I know where I am and what comes next. To the right of the road, the town of Philmont shows up itself on time as expected. In the distance, I see the Catskill Mountains. I bank to the left and set myself on the easterly heading.

According to my calculations and look at the sectional, I will be going over the Berkshire mountain range, and in the valley on the other side, I should see my airport.

It feels I am flying very close to the ground at 3,000 feet. I climb to 3,500. From this altitude, I can see the valley on the other side of the mountain. It is getting closer and closer. The terrain is falling. Some grassy fields open in front of me crossed by highways and roads I have never seen before. Also, there is a railroad track. I don't remember a railroad track on this side of the airport. Besides, there is no airport here. Instead, there is a small town with its main street and a few houses on both sides, plus some sports field with what looks like a large schoolhouse nearby.

As my brain starts processing what to do next, some unpleasant feeling of nervousness starts setting in. Should I call someone? What do I say? Where am I? Am I going to embarrass myself? Should I turn back and follow my route the way I came in? My sight suddenly rests on the ADF (automatic direction finder). Great Barrington has an NDB beacon on the field. The frequency is already tuned in on the receiver, and the ADF needle is pointing to my right.

Turning to the right to point in my instrument's direction, I realize I am flying along the railroad track. Not that far in front of me, I see the paper factory and town of Housatonic. I call UNICOM on my radio to discover that winds now are calm and nobody is in the traffic pattern. I am going to be using runway 29 again to land.

Great Barrington runway 29

"How was the flight?" I hear UNICOM in my headset.
"It was perfect!" I reply.

CHAPTER

3

How Do You Sell The Invisible?

Before you can spread your wings with your first student, you will need to have one. Besides all the philosophical and emotional aspects of flying, a flight instructor is also a businessman or businesswoman with all the elements that come with it. When bookkeeping, accounting, and filing taxes may be handled by someone else when you work for a flight school. Selling is always going to be your responsibility, but what are you going to be selling?

We can all remember our first flight, and most of us will remember it for the rest of our lives. Was it a pleasant one? It had to be since we went this way and decided to make a career out of that experience. I assume here that you are a certificated pilot. Why is it, then, that so many introductory flights become a one-time experience for so many potential students? I am now a manager of Flight Proficiency for the Experimental Aircraft Association. I worked as a chief flight instructor for some flight schools in the northeast during my aviation career. When I started my flight instructor profession, I worked for one of the largest flight schools in New York. I went through many different schools during my training, from very small to a national academy, and all of them left me with the same conclusions.

Because I have a business background, it's easy for me to see that there's a total lack of any business training in the process of becoming a CFI. Yes, being an instructor is about teaching and flying, but our success will depend, in large part, on our business skills.

Regardless of how we envision ourselves, a flight school is a service business. Some businesses sell financial services. Others sell plumbing services or car parts. We sell flight instruction services. And we have to sell to exist.

I came to the United States forty years ago as a political refugee from Communist Poland and became a citizen five years later. Over those four decades, I've noticed a sharp decline in customer service in our great country. We've replaced small business–style, high-quality customer service with an obsession with short-term savings and profits. We've forgotten about the long-term benefits of customer loyalty.

Most instructors are teachers. Some are good teachers, but few are great salesmen, businessmen, and marketers. Our current strategy is a simple one. We wait in our offices for someone to call. Most of the time, our callers are people who've received a gift certificate because someone else thought they would want to learn to fly. We make appointments with our new "leads" as soon as possible because we want to build as many hours as possible, and the sooner, the better. When our intro flight customer shows up, the weather isn't perfect, but we're used to it, and it gives us a chance to show our new customer what skilled pilots we are and that we're not afraid.

It does not matter that an introductory flight is a little more expensive; if you take time spent in the air, then an hour of "regular" dual. The flight school requires that we use the oldest and cheapest airplane, "just in case." If the new customer doesn't come back, we can pocket the extra few bucks for our troubles and "marketing expenses."

Off we go. We fly for thirty minutes. We smile at the prospect, and he or she tries to smile back, even though the only thing they can think of is getting back to the steady ground before the wings come off the airplane. Then we try to close the deal by selling them a private pilot start-up kit for $500. In response, we get the famous "I have to think about it." We shake hands and never see our "student" again. What went wrong?

Everything. Let's look at vacuum cleaner salespeople for a change. These timeless icons of the capitalist economy are people we secretly feared not because of what they are or have to sell but because we are afraid that we may not be able to say no to them. Those well-dressed individuals already have a rebuttal for everything we may say. They would show us the most expensive model in their product line, ready to sell us something less expensive but still useful and modern. While any canned sales pitch always insults my intelligence, and I never want to be pressured to make any decisions, there is an analogy to be drawn. After all, most people buy simply because they like the quality of the product and its presentation.

So how do you sell the invisible? Like any other product, even an invisible one must be packaged and presented in the best possible way. What do we sell? Is it a pilot certificate, training, flights? No. Like anyone else in the service industry, we sell ourselves, our personalities, professionalism, and knowledge. How should we sell it? Like any product on the market, you have three choices: the right product in an unattractive package, a lousy product in an attractive package, and a superior product in a beautiful package. In the first situation, you may have the best, but all those nice boxes will outshine your "brown bag." The product will sell once in the second situation, but the customer will never reach for it again. Only the last one is a win–win situation—the right product in an excellent package.

So what is our package? It's the way we present ourselves. It's the environment in which we will fly our potential customers. On the introductory flight, even the weather can change the students' experiences. Will they say "That was fun" or think (and tell their friends) "That was supposed to be fun? I'll never do that again!" It's also the feedback they receive from us on this first day. Catch them doing something right and let them know about it. Be honest, but look for a way to make a positive comment. It's their first time, but they must have some skills that look promising.

It's also the way we lead them to our best airplane. You may make a few dollars less on this one occasion, but it's cheap advertising. Compare this $10 or $20 to the cost of a simple display ad in a local newspaper or on the web. Then compare it to your profit when this student enrolls in your private pilot course: fifty hours of rental for just $20 in advertising looks good, doesn't it? And you'll leave them thinking that a school capable of having such good airplanes must be doing something right. Imagine walking into an attorney's office in an old broken-down trailer with a metal desk and two folding chairs. Would you do business with this lawyer? At the same time, be honest and explain that you may conduct training in a simpler, older airplane. But this is what they could look forward to when they are pilots and can rent or own their own. My recipe is a simple one: show that you're proud of your school and make new customers feel good about spending their money with you. Remember, flying is addictive, and all we have to do is make them have a positive experience.

CHAPTER

4

The Sky is Clear—My Personal Experience

It is one of those winter-fall days in the northeast. Trees already have lost their colors and stand naked and stark. There is no snow on the ground yet, but you can almost smell it in the air. You can feel it coming. Utica is a medium-sized class Delta controlled airport with somewhat sporadic traffic most of the time. There is some classic feel and look about this airfield with its long runways and relatively older hangars (one of them housing a DC-10), blue taxiway lights on the background of a red dawn sky. It is my favorite airport.

Author at one of the airports along the way

I am a new private pilot working on my multiengine rating and an aviation college degree. My experience of just a little over two hundred hours makes me feel like I can accomplish anything. I am very particular about all procedures, preflight and weather planning. As before any other flight, I start planning one of our standard cross-country school requirements. We are going to fly to Elmira and be back home just before dark.

A DUAT weather briefing with its coded information on a sizable amber tube monitor satisfies my legal requirement and does not show anything unusual. A slow cold front is well to our west, and there is no prediction for any lake-effect precipitation. Only lonely AIRMET Zulu (ice) gets my attention for a second, but the wording "in clouds" and a quick look at the sky and satellite screen puts all my worries aside. After all, the sky is clear!

Routine preflight does not demonstrate anything wrong. I know this old Seneca 1 very well by now, so my instructor feels more like a passenger than a second pilot. Perfect takeoff, handout to Griffis Departure, handover to Syracuse Approach, and then, "Seven-Five-Tango, could you check if you hear ELT signal on your radios?"

"Will do," I respond kindly and request frequency change. The 125.5 MHz does sing its emergency sound once strong and then very quiet like it is fading away. After relaying information to Syracuse, we are asked to check in, in few minutes again. Shortly we check again. The same sound, the same pattern; however, now we have problems communicating on one of our comm radios.

Suddenly, a brilliant idea turns on a bright light in my brain. "It must be our own ELT." After all, there are many problems that surface on many occasions in this relatively not-so-new airplane. After informing Syracuse Approach of our intentions and making a 180-degree turn, we land back in Utica to discover, to our big surprise, that the 121.5 MHz frequency is silent like it was never alive.

A quick look at all connections made me believe that whatever gremlins may have done here fixed itself, and they are a long time gone already. In the meantime, my favorite airport is starting to show its beauty, covering itself with a red blanket provided by the setting sun.

Officially, sunset is yet more than half an hour away, so I have to make my "aeronautical decision." Scientifically looking at the sky, more beautiful now than ever with just a few forming clouds, I say my verdict, "Let's go again!"

After all, we can fly at night.

Time to Elmira is so uneventful that it makes me think how airline pilots feel on much longer legs they have to fly. We land after sunset, but the darkness did not settle yet at this corner of the earth. The wind seems to start picking up its pace, blowing like someone who tries to blow candles on a birthday cake. Since it becomes apparent that we are not going to be back for any sort of "normal timed" dinner and know there are several good restaurants in this airport's vicinity, the decision is obvious. Food always plays an important part in my life. I have to admit, I have a little addiction to it.

We leave the restaurant well after dark. Commuter airplanes approaching to land with their strobes and position lights look very pretty in the background of a dark, almost black sky with a few stars shining like small holes in a blanket.

"Look, we can see stars!" I say, at the same time implying that it will be no problem with the flight back to our home airport.

We are going to a weather station at the airport to take a brief look at the radar screen. We want to be cautious, and we are "professionals." Little green and white spots on the screen move slowly to the east, but nothing that we cannot outrun.

"Seven-Five-Tango clear for takeoff...winds are...8 knots gusting 18." I feel that gust right after takeoff, but not a big deal. I am thinking, *Seven-Five-Tango is dancing the tango,* smiling to myself "how funny" I could be. Left turn, and we are going to climb to a proper altitude of 5,500. Correct takeoff power setting and good performance bring 3,500 in no time, and then it feels like someone just turned off the TV set and went to sleep. All outside visibility wholly and suddenly disappears.

I am well experienced in my instrument flying, so automatically and without any thinking, I rely on my instrument panel, but we are still climbing. Should we descend? How low are these clouds? Is it just some local cloud that we are going to pop out of in a few seconds? I look outside, and "the TV is still off." My eyes are attached now permanently to our "six-pack." All kinds of questions start wandering in my head. We are on a VFR flight!

I make my decision to try to descend at least to 2,500 feet. Before I can announce my thoughts, the sky opens itself with an indescribable beauty of its velvet blanket with millions of lights above the white carpet of fluff made of clouds. Smooth air makes me feel suspended in some unreal gigantic dome of a planetarium. So our problems are over. We are flying VFR and at our legal 5,500 as prescribed by the FAA.

We are talking to Syracuse Approach like nothing had happened. Handover to Griffis comes only as expected. In a calm, professional voice, I ask for IFR clearance to descend to UTICA, which has, according to ATIS, the above VFR minimums.

"Seven-Five-Tango, descend and maintain four thousand," I hear in my headset.

This request puts us right in the middle of our carpet of clouds. My eyes again glue themselves to an instrument panel. My instructor calmly hands me a flashlight.

"Look at the leading edge of your side..."

And there it is. I have seen it only on photographs in books and chapters about airplane icing. This one is real. It is hard for me to determine its thickness, but I can see it building up along with my excitement.

"Seven-Five-Tango, descend and maintain three thousand..."

Maybe that will help. I am not sure whether I am talking in my mind or expressing myself out loud. We seem to be in the middle of a layer.

Without asking the instructor's opinion, I say to my microphone, "Seven-Five-Tango, we are accumulating moderate rime ice. Need to descend as soon as possible."

Another quick look at my left wing with sizable ice coverage tells me that the situation is serious even though I don't feel any change in aircraft handling or performance, and then...

"Look ahead," I hear my instructor's voice.

His flashlight reveals a totally and entirely ice-covered windshield. At this time, my brain is full of articles I have read about landings with just looking to the side, but after all, I have only a little over two hundred hours.

The calm and peaceful face of my instructor gives me hope that he has done it "hundreds of times," hasn't he?

"Seven-Five-Tango, descend and maintain two thousand five hundred..."

Looking to the left, I can see that we are out of clouds. Ice on the leading edge seems to be holding firm. The windshield, however, starts showing small spots of visibility. Through the increasing holes that are rapidly thawing, I can see Utica's beacon behind falling flakes of light snow.

We land without saying any word. In silence, we taxi off the runway.

"Utica Tower, Seven-Five-Tango, we have experienced moderate ice in the clouds. Please let others know."

After all, we are "professionals."

That was years ago. I have accumulated many more hours since that time. There is no flight now that I would undertake without remembering that particular day.

CHAPTER

5

Fundamentals of Instructing

The Six Commandments

I remember it as if it were yesterday. Hot air radiates from a rock I am sitting on. The Nevada desert's slightly cooler air around me smells like sand if sand can have a smell. The air around me is not moving, and just the setting sun becomes dimmer and more crimson as it sets on the horizon after a full day of work.

I can still hear the voice in my head.

"Congratulations! Here is your instructor certificate!"

I want to shout from the surrounding mountaintops that look like a landscape on the surface of the moon. I keep repeating in my head, *I am a flight instructor!* My lifelong dream just became a reality.

After the subcontracting to the college flight school went bankrupt and closed abruptly on the day I was supposed to have my multiengine check ride, I started roaming various small schools in the northeast to complete my certificates. Finally, I decided to go to Las Vegas, Nevada, to complete my instructor's credentials.

Now I am unable anymore to count all my students over the years. There were so many of them. Names and faces have been blurred over time, but the satisfaction always remains the same. They were all the best friends for me, and they all took with them my experience and love to fly to embody them in their ideals and achievements. I hope they pass them on to the next generations of pilots as well.

My students' success measures my success. When I have time, I will carve this sentence on some wood and hang it in my office on the wall. Perhaps I will also make a few extra and give them to every flight instructor I meet. From this sentence, I was starting every first lesson with each CFI student I trained. Just as a child's first independent steps or a first spoken word is a parent's great joy, so too will the success and achievement of a CFI's disciple make a real teacher happy.

All this didn't come on its own, and there is science behind education. Unfortunately, as some of my aviation teachers told me during my aviation college training days, we need to memorize some terminology, acronyms, and get that Fundamentals of Instructing (FOI) test out of the way so it will not "interfere" with my CFI training. There are no words to describe how quickly I have discovered how wrong it was.

★ ★ ★

Don't worry! This book is not about recycling textbook knowledge. I am not going to give you another acronym to remember. We are not going to memorize definitions. However, we will look at the practical application of those elements and their importance.

For me, the flight instructor training would consist solely of those elements we find in the Fundamentals of Instructing book. After all, all flight instructor candidates are already instrument-rated commercial pilots who should possess all the necessary aviation knowledge. Transition to the right seat is challenging but can be done relatively quickly. And now should be the time to learn how to teach.

The six laws of learning are critical in your career. You probably remembered them at some point if you are a CFI. Or maybe you just try to memorize them as you read this book and study to be a CFI. They are as follows:

- Law of readiness
- Law of primacy
- Law of intensity
- Law of effect
- Law of exercise
- Law of recency

As you most likely noticed, I didn't list them in the order they are usually presented. If you try to remember them, RPIEER, it doesn't mean anything. You will not memorize it easily. So don't! I listed them in a logical sequence. Let's look at it first before we analyze each one individually.

So what is the sequence? It is, in fact, applicable to all learning scenarios. Firstly, one has to be READY and want to learn. When they come in, they will be exposed to the aviation environment and you as their teacher for the FIRST time. It is going to be an unforgettable, INTENSE experience, whether it was positive or negative. What they will do with you will have some EFFECTS. If the experience was positive, they would repeat it over and over to EXERCISE what they discovered. If they take an extended break and have not done it RECENTLY, they will forget. Now you can see where I am going with it. As you have probably guessed by now, I am a firm believer in logic and understanding instead of memorizing definitions.

Now let's take a look at each one individually with some examples. I would have a long list of illustrations I could offer you in this book, but I am sure you can come up with your own based on what I will show you.

The Law of Readiness

You may have heard or read about the law of readiness explained as a need for students to have their basic needs like food, health, and adequate sleep satisfied. It is true, but with a significant simplification. The real essence of this law lies somewhere else. If the student has no desire to learn to fly, they may never show up and you will never see them at all. Of course, some of us are born with a yearning to be in the air. But it is totally up to you to inspire the desire for those who will come to you by some course of curiosity or other aspiration. And here, you will need to be honest.

How many times have you heard "Driving to the airport is more dangerous than flying"? Every time we go flying, we think of our flight as being the safe one. We have done all the mandatory briefings, have obtained all pertinent information, and have done our preflight. And yet accident rates in general aviation have stayed obstinately unchanged, and the fatality rate hangs just over one death every one hundred thousand hours per NTSB. GA aircraft has a fatality rate of about nineteen times greater than driving. Maybe the problem is that we have been lying to ourselves and others for years and saying out loud "Flying GA is and is going to be risky" is not such a bad idea after all.

Some of you will most likely scream here, "But, Radek, who will want to do such a dangerous and risky activity? We have to make it safe!" My prediction is, when we are honest, more people will come than you think.

Maslow's order of needs, which I will be addressing in more detail later in this book, is a concept in psychology proposed by Abraham Maslow in his 1943 paper "A Theory of Human Motivation." It states that "self-actualization" is the highest level of human need and our ultimate desire. This level refers to what a person's full potential is and the realization of that potential. In other words, it is in our nature to want to accomplish things.

When we define accomplishment as the achievement of a task, the more challenging and riskier the task, the higher is the level of satisfaction. We undertake dangerous activities starting in our childhood with climbing trees or learning how to travel on only two wheels. And when many may settle in life with satisfaction derived from less risky accomplishments, some of us will always push for the ultimate.

Would we go rock climbing having the assurance of 100 percent safety? Would we go skiing knowing that it does not require any skill to concur? Would we descend to a dark cave knowing what is there and being assured of absolute protection? Would you become a police officer knowing that you will never have to face a challenging situation? Would you join the army? All those activities require acquired skills, training, practice, risk assessment, and risk management. And that is precisely why we are doing them. Not because they are safe but because they are risky. I will argue that eliminating the risk factor in the above would significantly diminish those activities' attractiveness. The same would happen in general aviation. But the risk does not have to be dangerous. I will argue that we fly exactly because general aviation is not safe and requires a significant level of skill, learning, and accomplishment.

So do not be afraid to say to your potential student, "General aviation flying is risky." It is precisely why we are doing it, knowing that proper risk management will not allow it to become dangerous. I guarantee you that you will challenge your prospective client enough to be READY to learn.

The Law of Primacy

It is a relatively straightforward concept. I am not going to say anything new here.

According to the FAA, "Primacy, the state of being first, often creates a strong, almost unshakable impression and underlies the reason an instructor must teach correctly the first time and the student must learn correctly the first time" (FAA

2009, p. 2–11). What is acknowledged here is very simple: what we learn first, we know best. But this rule is actually much broader than you think. It is not only about teaching. You could be following all the proper procedures and do your checklists flawlessly, but still, you probably don't utilize this learning law to its full extent.

You probably have heard the saying "There is no second chance to make the first impression." No, I am not going to talk here about your dress or personal hygiene. I always believe that teaching something so obvious is insulting to anyone who wants to be a professional in any career in life. Just make sure you are not going to try to be somebody else. Be yourself. And if you are an honest and good person caring about others, it will show on its own. If you are not, you shouldn't be where you are.

A long time ago, at one of the flight schools where I served as a chief flight instructor, I required all my flight instructors to be honest and sincerely caring about their students. I asked one of the student clients who traveled thousands of miles from Poland why she wanted to learn to fly there. What was her first impression?

★ ★ ★

Twenty-four-year-old Maria (or, as we call her, Marysia) Kayser arrives at our school in early July. From the very beginning, she is spreading a good sense of humor throughout the airport.

"I've always dreamed of flying," she says. "But everyone always looked at me as if I wanted to achieve something impossible."

Dreams turned to plans when Maria worked as a babysitter for pilots and the Royal Air Force members in Scotland. They are the ones who took her to air shows, showed her planes and talked about flying.

"I liked it, and they showed me that dreams are possible to achieve," says Maria.

"Why the USA?" I ask out of curiosity.

A small moment of hesitation shows up on her face.

"I read a lot about training abroad in *PILOT* magazine [Polish general aviation magazine, RW]. I wondered about the States. I was also thinking about Australia, but it didn't look so well organized," she says, a little embarrassed, as if she were admitting doing something wrong once she thinks about Australia.

"So what do you think about our flight school?" I ask.

"I honestly thought that it would be different. I was surprised by the extraordinary friendliness of the staff and instructors. People are open, calm, and very cordial."

"What do you think about the training program?" I ask.

"What I like the most is that we fly almost from the very beginning of training. I can check academic knowledge almost immediately in practice. An individual training course with an instructor allows you to learn details and ask questions during ground lessons. Planes are available almost anytime, so I can fly at will as the weather allows. I also like the fact that the training takes place at a busy airport. Admittedly, you have to work a lot on communication in English, but I like it. I like that you can also fly with many different instructors, as you want to see different training styles. All CFIs are high-class professionals and experts. Everyone can explain everything well, although in a different way. And everything is so well organized. You can also fly at will in the back seat during the training of other students. One can learn a lot only by observing," she says.

In just a few weeks of training, Marysia solos without much trouble on a Cessna 172. I ask how her first solo flight is.

The radiant smile lights up my office with indescribable rays.

"It was GREAT!" she replies. "I was a little nervous at the beginning, but I found out that after good training, I can fly."

★ ★ ★

As you probably noticed, this story is full of positive first impressions. From the first impression of being exposed to air shows in Scotland. From the first impression of reading an article about how well the flight training is organized to meeting honest professionals and a smiling crew. As you can see, it is not only how you can dress or look. The law of PRIMACY takes the entire team of people to be entirely successful, but results will be gratifying, and the references you will get will be endless. I hope you derive a few more ideas from the story above—the ideas I am not exploring due to this paragraph's different scope. I am sure they can and will be useful for you to implement in your flight instructor career.

Now let us move to the next law on our list.

The Law of Intensity

The intensity principle suggests that a client will learn more from the genuine thing than from an alternative. But as always, there is much more to it.

Can you tell me what you were doing on Tuesday two weeks ago at 14:15, your local time? Unless something special happened on that day or you are a genius born with an incredible memory, most likely your answer will be "no."

Let's define this "something special." If you tripped and fell on your face that day, you probably will remember, but it will be something that you may want to forget. If the event was very traumatic, your brain might even help you here by suppressing that memory. On the other hand, if you were looking at that time at your TV screen to discover you hold a winning lottery ticket in your hand, you probably will remember that for a long time. Of course, both examples are extremes to illustrate the point. And the matter is that we remember moments, events, or whole days if they are unique or out of the ordinary in a positive way.

Don't be afraid to be creative, and you will be rewarded with your student catching on with their learning process flawlessly. By injecting some humor when appropriate, you may easily create those small "intense" yet positive moments.

When you are in an airplane like a Cessna or Warrior, with one of your primary students during the first lesson, you encounter their first challenge—how to remember that the yoke is not a steering wheel. Of course, we could just explain, but as we will discover shortly, it will take some time for your student to remember. Can we safely create an "intense" and joyous moment in such a dull phase of flight? The technique I have been using is very simple.

★ ★ ★

After spending about an hour in the pre-briefing room and reviewing what our flight will look like and what we will be learning today, I take my student to do a meticulous preflight, demonstrating how we do it and what they can expect to do in the future. The wind is calm, and the sky is clear. You couldn't have asked for better weather. I demonstrate the start-up process, and now is the time to taxi.

"Let me demonstrate how it works," I say.

I take the yoke in my hand, and at the time, as I am turning it to the left, I unnoticeably press on the left rudder pedal, then the same thing to the right. After this, what you may think a rather peculiar exercise, I give the controls to my student, of course, doing our standard briefed-before-the-flight, exchange-of-controls procedure.

"Now you try it," I declare.

We move slowly forward as I maintain firm control of the throttle. My student turns the yoke to the left. Nothing happens. Now they turn it to the right. As expected, still nothing.

"It doesn't work!" I hear them saying.

"Exactly! My controls!" I respond as I gently push on the brakes. "Let me show you how it is really done," I say with a smile. We laugh a little, and we proceed with the real demonstration and exercise.

From that point forward, every time my student's hand wonders to the yoke to turn it like a steering wheel, they look at me, smile, and say, "I remember!" And they abandon their action. The event is positively intense enough to stay with them for the rest of their training and, I hope, for the rest of their life.

★ ★ ★

Of course, it comes without saying that you need to plan such an approach considering all the safety aspects of your environment and flight phases. You can create many "intense and positive" elements on the ground or at a safe altitude. But also, the entire flight may and should be unforgettable.

★ ★ ★

It was years ago, but I still remember it as if it were yesterday. It is the middle of summer, and flying reminds me of being in a sauna. High humidity is causing not only above-average and challenging-to-endure temperatures but also limited visibility. I fly in something that resembles a milk soup.

Just in case, when I practice maneuvers with my students, I always request a radar following from our local controllers. Legally, we are still above VFR minimums, but in practice, it looks different. But we must fly. My student is sweating trying to repeat the maneuver I just demonstrated. I am sweating because it is hot, and I am continually paying attention so the student will not kill both of us. And this is what I like. Life can be so beautiful.

It is still hot. The temperature is exceeding all norms of common sense. Thirty degrees Celsius, forty degrees Celsius. The air is resembling a steam room. Visibility is limited to just a few miles. The propeller is grinding the air like it was turning in space. When we start moving forward, the runway's gray stretch moves slowly under us as it is trying to overcome its laziness. Slowly, like a large train locomotive, we climb up in the air. Earth is escaping and becoming smaller. Hangars shrink gradually, and cars in the parking lot are becoming children's toys. The air is smooth like butter. Even the slightest breeze is not disturbing our climb on a quiet, invisible road up to the sky.

All problems are disappearing, left behind, and becoming small and insignificant. Once more, I look down. Being a pilot is one of the greatest professions in the world. What would I do if I could not fly? This is my very personal "intense" moment.

Every flight makes humans free. A night flight makes a human free and aware of the beauty of the world. As we take off from the Kline Kill Airport's grass strip in Ghent, New York, the airplane is happily jumping up and down on the grassy terrain's uneven texture below as it is predicting some incredible adventure in its immediate future. Horizontal stabilizer held all the way aft is positioning us quickly in the ground-effect pillow just a few feet above the ground. We are slowly accelerating to the rotation speed. Vx (best angle of climb) comes in no time. Another small pull on the yoke is triggering the green surface to flee below. Telephone wires on the right side of the runway abruptly move downward. Our Cessna 172 is majestically rising in the air. On the left side, the sun's bashful red face is hiding behind the Catskill Mountains in the west. We turn on course, banking to the right. The splendor of the sunset is left behind us. In front of us, the deep, dark void demonstrates itself with just a few small sparks like a dying campfire left alone behind by tourists.

The night should be like a dark crystal, not a velvet; a weird notion comes through my mind. High humidity is making the darkness almost touchable. We are climbing to 5,500 feet. With light anxiety, which I am successfully hiding from my student, I study the sectional in my flashlight's red light. It isn't easy in reddish illumination to recognize symbols on the map. I do not know what a city is and what is a lake. They both look the same, but one should be yellow and the other blue. I can help myself with the GPS that I have in my flight bag, but I will not embarrass myself here. Once more, I look in front of us. With huge relief, I see the large group of lights. I look at my watch. Just as planned, we are above Pittsfield, Massachusetts. Not long after that, we leave behind and in our distant right lights of the town of Westfield. All the other waypoints come and go as planned.

I am imagining that we are tracking hunters who leave unextinguished campfires behind. Suddenly, the pulsating green-and-white light of the airport's beacon appears on the horizon.

My student, without a word, turns on the carburetor heat and is reducing the power. The airplane is slowly falling into the abyss of darkness. We call the tower and get clearance to land as "number 2" behind some lonely at this hour-lost commuter. The green, white, and red lights of the runway markings are happily blinking our welcome. To my surprise, I look at my watch; one hour and fifteen minutes passed in no time. Canyons of streets appear below us with little crawling lights inside them. On the right, I see a group of stores brightly lit with some red neon signs. The airplane is gently kissing the smoothness of the concrete of the large runway of our destination airport. The world is returning to its real size. The velvet of night is left once again high above.

★ ★ ★

The Law of Effect

Learning requires the pattern of relationships, and relationships are reinforced or weakened according to the law of effect. The law states that behaviors that lead to rewarding outcomes are likely to be repeated, though actions that lead to undesired results are less likely to repeat.

I just wrote above something that sounds very scientific and "intelligent." That is not my intention in this book. Let's take a look yet again at the real meaning behind this law, its very close relation to Maslow's hierarchy of needs, and its practical aspects.

On the surface, the law of effect is very straightforward. If we like the results of our actions, we will do it again. If we don't, we will try to avoid doing what caused those unpleasant results. But how does it relate to Maslow's theory and the practical life?

If you are a CFI, you most likely have heard about Maslow's pyramid.

Maslow's hierarchy of needs is a concept in psychology that consists of a five-level human needs model, often shown as hierarchical layers within a pyramid. Though some research suggests that Maslow never invented a pyramid to exemplify the hierarchy of needs, I will not challenge those theories here because Maslow's theory remains popularly supported by its broadly recognized pyramid form. And it is widely presented in aviation education this way. From the bottom of the pyramid up, the needs are biological (food and clothing), safety (security), fitting in (friendship), esteem, and self-actualization (accomplishment). According to Maslow, needs lower down in the hierarchy must be satisfied before individuals can attend to higher needs. Here is when I am going to disagree partially. Let's take a look at Maslow's pyramid itself first (fig. 1).

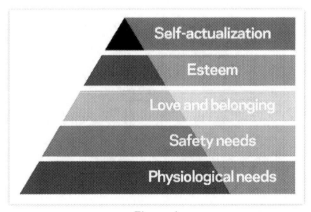

Figure 1

If we start from the bottom, the first layer is addressing every basic need, and it is often portrayed in the aviation training books as the need of your student not to be hungry and be dressed appropriately. What if we cut this tier out (fig. 2)?

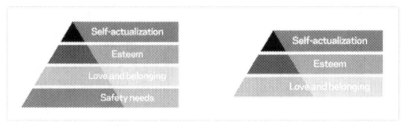

Figure 2

Can a hungry individual learn if they want to? I know they can. My parents and their friends went through years of the German occupation of Poland. They were hungry and continuously afraid for their lives, but they finished underground schools and got their diplomas. We can keep cutting those layers, and to our surprise, we will discover that we can learn if we don't feel safe, loved, or accepted by our peers. But what happens if we start cutting from the top (fig. 3)?

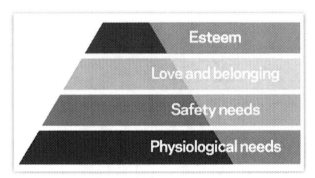

Figure 3

Now we have a problem. Picture yourself in training that does not result in any accomplishment. Or a school you go to but never receive any diploma. Perhaps a flight training course that will get you ready to fly by yourself but will never allow you to solo. How about a private pilot course that does not result in you getting your private pilot certificate? By now, I am sure you see where I am going with it. The highest and the most critical layer is at the top of the pyramid. As humans, we can make sacrifices, but we are unable to exist without an accomplishment. We can all also agree that accomplishment, defined by the dictionary as "something that has been achieved successfully," is a positive outcome.

In summary, the most positive element of our flight training is an achievement. As long as your students will be accomplishing something in every lesson, they will be coming back for more. I always made sure that every session with my students right from the very first intro flight had its own, as I call it, wow factor. No matter how small it was going to be. It could be as simple as the ability to lift off from a runway without any CFI help or a discovery, why we perform specific procedures, what is behind it, how it works, and seeing results of their action. As I call it, the WHY checklist.

I began my flight instructing career at a large flight school in the northeast. My office was in a shared space with another instructor. Our flight school also used that room for flight preparations and examinations. When an examiner and a student occupied the room, I would go to roam the vast space of this airport so that the exam could take place in full privacy. That room was my home away from home. In that room, I held many interesting conversations about aviation and the pursuits of life in general.

One day a pilot who was in the process of obtaining his CFI certificate shared with me his experience from a recent check ride with an examiner. He was a good pilot; he was a commercial, instrument-rated pilot with substantial flying experience. After a satisfactory oral and flight examination, he performed one of the aircraft securing phase checklist items known as the mag ground check. We can argue the need for it. There have been endless discussions about the benefits and disadvantages of this procedure, but his examiner popped in a simple question, "If you do it, then why?"

Even though he had performed hundreds of magneto checks (this particular school required them as a school policy), no one had ever explained why they were done. He knew the proper procedure and outcome of the magneto checks very well; he knew what to look for and what to expect for proper operation, but he didn't understand the system and therefore did not comprehend the magneto's mechanical process check nor what an improper reading meant.

Somehow, throughout all his training, no one thought it was important to explain each checklist item's purpose or they assumed he already knew the answer or perhaps none of his instructors knew the answers themselves. It is evident in other areas of aviation education as well. Many students whom I have questioned during their stage checks were able to verify items listed on their checklist for proper operation. However, they were not able to explain the purpose of the procedure. An excellent example of this I also see with the instrument students. They can check to see whether the alternate static source is operating correctly, but they do not fully understand what it does.

Simple tasks after landing, such as "Strobes OFF" or "Transponder to STANDBY," are on the list for a reason. Consequently, every instructor and pilot should be ready to answer the question, "why?" Can you imagine getting into your car, pulling out the checklist, and performing the task "Ignition key, TURN" without knowing why you do it? Why then do we allow ourselves as pilots to perform blind tasks just to check them off? Think next time you say, "Ready for takeoff." Are you ready indeed?

I was lucky to be trained by one of the best teachers in the industry. My instructor gave me much of my knowledge between tasks, as oral quizzing or simple hangar talk, which made my learning a lot of fun. His influence helped me develop my addition to the official flight school's syllabus. I called it the why test.

Each airplane has its own set of checklists for different phases of flight. I break each list into chapters, for example, "Before Engine Start," "Engine Start," "Before Taxi," etc. In the early stages of the learning process, I would introduce a new section at the beginning of each flight lesson. We discussed each item in detail so students will clearly understand why they were performing each task. I held those lessons as casual conversations rather than formal lectures.

In many cases, the students didn't even realize that any formal training was taking place. I expected that each of them would explain every item on any checklist in the airplane before signing them off for any stage check or a check ride. It is essential that each pilot thoroughly understands the aircraft before becoming a pilot in command.

After-landing items such as "Carburetor heat OFF" may not save our lives, but it will protect our engine. The item "Strobes OFF" will preserve the night vision of other pilots nearby and make our workload less challenging.

On the other hand, knowing why we turn on the electric fuel pump before landing and takeoff may one day save our life when the mechanical pump fails. If we understand why we do it, we won't forget to do it, even if we cannot read the checklist in the dim light of a dark cockpit.

I want to encourage you to take the checklist from one of the airplanes you fly and put yourself through the why test. If you do, would you pass it? And when you do, isn't it going to be a significant, positive, and pleasant EFFECT?

The Law of Exercise

According to the *Oxford Dictionary of Sport Science and Medicine* (published online in 2008, eISBN: 9780191727788), the law of exercise is "a law which states that, in learning, the more frequently a stimulus and response are associated with each other, the more likely the particular response will follow the stimulus. The law implies that one learns by doing, and one cannot learn a skill, for instance, by watching others. It is necessary to practice the skill because by doing so, the bond between stimulus and response is strengthened. In applying this to motor learning, the more often a given movement is repeated, the more firmly established it becomes." Sounds impressive?

Yes, it does. Let's simplify it a little and show some practical applications.

Are you ready for an exercise? I want you to take a piece of paper. Ask one of your friends, spouse, or significant other to write down a three-digit number not related to anything in your life. Look at it once and put it away. Two days later, try to recall that number from your memory. If you can, I am impressed, but I will bet that you will not remember it. Now part 2. Take the same number and try to memorize it by looking at it every hour throughout the day. When you wake up the next morning, most likely, you will be able to repeat it from memory. Now put it away and don't look at it for a week. We will be talking about it when we cover our law number 6.

As we know, motor skills need to be practiced, but our brain also needs some constant exercise. My routine always was to voice every action in the cockpit or during preflight verbally. Why? Because this way, I don't have to pay attention if my student gets enough repetition exercise of what the action should be. And if I am by myself, I create my own challenge-response system. Of course, you should transfer this responsibility of exercise to your student at some point in the training as you gradually transfer the decision-making process. As you can see, repetition is a great EXERCISE.

The Law of Recency

And here we have arrived at the end of our list of the "six education commandments." The answer and explanation are enclosed within the name of this law itself. Remember that piece of paper with a number you tried to memorize? If you did put that note away for a week as I asked you to, you probably don't remember what was on it. Don't then expect your student to remember something you told her or him a few weeks or months ago. Don't be afraid to repeat yourself regularly.

CHAPTER

6

Effective Communication

According to FAA (*Aviation Instructor's Handbook*, FAA-H-8083-9), communication occurs when one person transmits ideas or feelings to another person or group of people. The effectiveness of the communication is measured by the similarity between the idea transmitted and the idea received.

The path of any interaction is comprised of three components:

- Source
- Symbols transmitting the message
- Receiver

I want you, my reader, to know those elements fully, but not in the sense of scientific definitions and complicated language. We need to understand them in a practical sense, and only then will we be able to apply our understanding in an aviation education career.

Aviation, in general, not just aviation radio communication, is a language of its own. Pilots and instructors communicate with each other and air traffic controllers (ATC), utilizing standard phraseology throughout the world. We expose our students to acronyms like ATIS, ASOS, ATC, etc. from the first lesson in training. It can cause substantial barriers in communication if not appropriately handled.

English happens to be the universal language used in aviation. After Polish, English is my second language. Some people might think that learning the aviation language is more difficult if English isn't their primary language due to the fast pace and specialized phrases, aside from the fact that it is in their second language. As a flight instructor, I have had an opportunity to watch new pilot students sweat through their first few hours in an airplane communicating with ATC. Many pilots have difficulty with common traffic advisory frequency (CTAF) and related traffic announcements. These pilots try to use memorized phrases, scripts, and textbook formulas to communicate.

If you understand what needs to be communicated, then the focus on memorizing becomes unnecessary.

Some may feel that I have unorthodox teaching methods; however, if you comprehend the principles of learning, you will realize that understanding is a level of knowledge that should come first before its application regarding teaching anything in life and aviation in particular. It does also apply to aviation radio communications, which I will cover later in this chapter. When learning a new language, we should learn how to speak it first before analyzing and formulating it.

I came to the United States from Poland almost four decades ago. The only language experience I had before was through textbooks in high school and college English classes. I could recognize sentence structure and was able to form phrases but was not able to communicate. I was not able to speak or understand even after years of structured training. It was only from real-life practice that I learned to express information effectively. I believe that textbook instruction is necessary for a proper foundation. Still, unfortunately, too many times, this is where we, as flight instructors, stop when it comes to teaching our students.

Let's look at those three basic elements of communication in the aviation education environment. The first and last are very straightforward. Sometimes you are the source and your student is the receiver; other times, it is the other way around. We communicate by speaking, waving our hands, or raising our eyebrows, among others. Sometimes your student's eyes will show a total absence of interest or understanding. Those are all the clues that you need to be able to pick up, understand, and use appropriately as a part of the communication process. As a teacher, you need to be sensitive to the smallest and most subtle signals your student could be communicating. If you miss them, a significant breakdown in communication will happen.

In the middle of all this, we have symbols transmitting the message. You may think, *OK, we speak the same language.* But do we?

To fully appreciate this "language barrier," let's look at the most common obstacles to effective communication. I am going to set aside the obvious once called external factors when the message is just not sent or received correctly (hearing problem, noise, etc.) and concentrate on something that we call lack of common experience. I call it the aviation language barrier.

If you speak Polish, please ask someone to insert below a different phrase from another language you don't know.

If I say out loud, "Dzień Dobry! Jak się masz?" and both of us are in the same quiet room, the message was sent. You have heard what I have said, so the message was received, but you still don't know what I have said. Of course, you can always memorize that sentence and repeat it. You can even translate it and discover that I said, "Good morning! How are you?" But it still doesn't mean you speak the language.

Be mindful when you say to your potential student on their first intro flight, "We will tune AWOS first and then switch to CTAF and talk to UNICOM for COMM CHECK. We will depart via CROSSWIND to our practice area."

It may sound obvious to you. For them, it is going to be, "Nic z tego nie rozumiem!"

I will let you find the translation of this one on your own.

Now let's move to the other area of aviation communication—the radio. Remember the law of primacy from the previous chapter? Your student is going to watch how you do it, and if it is done correctly from the beginning, it will stay with them for life the right way.

Ninety-seven percent of the knowledge required to communicate on the radio comes from knowing what information we are trying to relay, why it is essential to share this information, and how we should transmit this data. The other 3 percent comes from knowing how to be efficient with the actual words used in the transmission to minimize airtime. Of course, we still have the source (you or your student) and the receiver (ATC). But understanding the information that others will be expecting from us will make it easier to communicate. We share one particular frequency with many other pilots, whether it is on an air traffic control (ATC) frequency, common traffic advisory frequency (CTAF), or universal communications station (UNICOM). Time is not limitless, so it is crucial to communicate the information in the least amount of time to ensure proper aircraft separation.

When a pilot understands an air traffic controller's job, his understanding of radio communication becomes clear. Once you know what information needs to be relayed, it can be done in more than one format. It is wise to maintain a professional manner when transmitting information because it reduces the chances of ambiguity or obscurity and the need for repetition. However, there are many variations from students to experienced pilots, which can be refined to improve communications and decrease airtime. I observe the most variations at the hold-short line to the departure runway where the pilot reports at a towered airport.

Here is one of the "towered" examples:

- Transmission 1: XYZ Tower, Warrior 123AB.
- Transmission 2: Warrior 123AB, XYZ Tower.

- Transmission 3: XYZ Tower, Warrior 123AB, short of runway 20, is ready for takeoff. We will be departing to the northwest.
- Transmission 4: 3AB cleared for takeoff 2-0.
- Transmission 5: Warrior 123AB cleared for takeoff on runway 20.

I timed this conversation. It took precisely forty-five seconds. If you think forty-five seconds is not a long time, listen to any radio commercial. They are thirty to sixty seconds long and seem to drag on forever. During the time it took the Warrior to get clearance for takeoff, another aircraft that the tower previously instructed to report 3-mile final to the same runway for landing could not report its position. There is a reason why I called it a conversation. Conversations are very different from communications. A conversation is a dialog, an informal interchange of thoughts, whereas communication is transmitting facts.

Let's analyze the first line: "XYZ Tower, Warrior 123AB."

The Warrior has just left the ground frequency, having just taxied over various taxiways to the active runway and is reporting into the tower. It is not necessary to get the tower's attention at this time. They know your call sign and your position. In fact, at many smaller Class D airports, the tower controller will be the same person you just spoke with on the ground control frequency. The tower is waiting for you to tell them something useful, for example, that you are ready for departure or that, conversely, you forgot something and need to return to your point of origin on the airfield.

Let's now take a look at the second line: "Warrior 123AB, XYZ Tower."

Tower would not have been required to say this if the Warrior hadn't used the first sentence to announce their presence. As you can see, more valuable airtime was used unnecessarily.

How can line 3 be refined to be more efficient? "XYZ Tower, Warrior 123AB, short of runway 20, is ready for takeoff. We will be departing to the northwest."

When you stop at the hold-short line, it is vital to listen for a few seconds after switching to tower frequency, or anytime you change frequencies, to prevent interrupting someone else's communication. Then announce, "3AB ready 2-0, northwest departure."

Removing unnecessary words makes communications clear and concise. Verbiage at this stage that is redundant includes the aircraft type and position and the intentions to take off at the end of the runway. It is also good practice to shorten the aircraft's call sign to the last three characters once you've established communications with each frequency. When you get your clearance, restate, "3AB cleared for takeoff 2-0."

I timed this shortened communication too; it took ten seconds.

Let's apply the same concept to our nontowered field. First, we should consider the famous *W*'s: who, where, and what.

Who are we?

We can answer this question in a few different ways, so we have to apply common sense and logic to determine the best way to respond depending on our environment's needs. It is vital to announce precisely who we are, our aircraft type and identification, in a controlled environment. It is more important to identify ourselves by our size and speed in an uncontrolled environment than our tail number. Think about it this way. When ATC announces traffic to you, would it be more important to know whether N4900H or N5137B is a factor to you or that a Cessna 152 versus a regional jet is at your twelve o'clock passing you at 1,000 feet above? When a pilot visually scans the sky, it is easier to find an aircraft if we know what type to look for. So when you are communicating in a nontowered environment, identify yourself by the aircraft type. A King Air 200, 10 miles to the west, versus a Cessna 172, in the same location, makes a big difference. With this information, you will also know when to expect the other aircraft to arrive in the traffic pattern.

To whom are we talking?

I have heard so many variations that it would be difficult to list them all. Some examples include UNICOM, RADIO, area traffic, and even tower. In an uncontrolled environment, we are addressing anyone that is on the same frequency. Remember that many airports can share one frequency. It is essential to address other aircraft in your vicinity as a group. The traffic within one airport should be addressed by that airport's name, for example, Newport Traffic.

Where are we?

There is only one proper way to identify an aircraft's location. First, remember that we are flying in a three-dimensional space. Second, realize that the other pilots you are speaking to may not be familiar with the area that they are flying in. Understanding these points will help you recognize that landmarks such as shopping malls, lakes, highways, or buildings could confuse someone new to the area. Information that is universal and can create a precise picture includes distance, direction, and altitude.

"North Central Traffic, King Air, six west, three thousand, descending inbound 32" gives a more precise image to a pilot about the traffic than "Northampton Unicom, 98795, maneuvering over marina." The first communication information enables a pilot to determine the traffic's location and approximate speed and intended course of action.

What are we going to be doing?

Here, our options are simple. When you approach any airport, think about what you would want to know from that other visiting or coming-home aircraft. I want to know if it will be doing full-stop landing, stop-and-go, or maybe touch-and-go. I also want to know if it will be remain in the traffic pattern or going to the ramp. At some airports, that may influence your taxi route if you are ready to go to the runway. I want to know all the information that will allow me to adjust what I am doing for a proper and safe separation between me and anybody else in the neighborhood. As an example, we could say "Inbound, full stop" or "Inbound, touch-and-go, staying in the pattern."

Applying this simple understanding of how to communicate with reducing our verbiage to the basics will allow us to sound like professional airline pilots or maybe even better within just a few hours.

CHAPTER

7

Defense Mechanisms

As humans, we react to our environment. When we feel cold, we cover ourselves. When we see objects being thrown in our direction, we duck to avoid them. The biological defense mechanism is a bodily reaction that protects or preserves beings. But the defense mechanisms can also be purely psychological.

As we have determined in previous chapters, the most desirable human need is the need for accomplishment. And we are not willing to give up that accomplishment very quickly. When things are not going our way, we "lie" first to others and then ourselves. We subconsciously tell ourselves, "It is impossible I did this wrong. Something else caused me to do it that way." When we trip on a carpet, we blame the rug rather than the fact that we were not watching where we were going.

There are many defense mechanisms you encounter, but the most common are the following:

- Repression
- Denial
- Compensation
- Projection

- Rationalization
- Aggression

No, I didn't list them all here. Here are the ones I have seen most in my near two decades of being a CFI. If you desire a more formal and complete list, you will find it in the *Aviation Instructor's Handbook* (FAA-H-8083-9). Some of those listed above are easy to recognize, like aggression or rationalization, but some are very difficult to detect, like repression. All of them are almost impossible to deal with after the fact. That is why it is essential to anticipate them or notice them ahead of their occurrence. You will be able to disarm them just like undetonated explosives before they even surface.

★ ★ ★

I am flying with my students out of Norwood Memorial Airport in Massachusetts. A very nice medium-sized Delta towered airport with two crossing runways and a very long ramp housing many single-engine aircraft of three flight schools located on this field along runway 35. Since the airport is located right under Boston's Bravo airspace, we need to "crawl" from under it to the southeast to our practice area about 15 miles away.

It's the middle of summer. The air is warm and thick like honey, and we are all looking forward to climbing up to cooler temperatures above and to be behind this big fan attached to the engine of the flight school's Cessna 172. There is no better air-conditioning than that. The day comes to an end, but the sun is still high, and the temperature is still being elevated. My only concern is the potential of thunderstorms that may build up later on, but so far, the forecast looks good, and the air is still smooth.

John, a young guy in his twenties who wants to be an airline pilot, is always in a good mood. His bright, intelligent eyes are showing high interest in everything we cover in training. Today's flight will be his first introduction to instrument flying under the hood. He is still in the first phase of his private pilot course but is almost ready to solo.

We "sweat" our preflight. Although I am watching to make sure we are not going to crash due to a mechanical failure, he is doing all the work looking at each bolt and nut as prescribed by the checklist. Engine start brings, perhaps just in our imagination, a little cooling effect. The airplane smells like most student abused aircraft; a mix of oil and aviation fuel, with a bit of an old upholstery aroma. Taxi and takeoff go without a glitch. I don't have to correct or even hover over controls. We are sitting in the middle of the practice area, looking around in no time. But it seems like we are there alone. Two clearing turns in the opposite direction give us some sense of security. Now comes the time to go under the hood.

John arms himself in what is officially called an aviation view-limiting device. We covered in our ground lesson before this flight precisely what we are going to be doing. John, without hesitation, follows my instructions almost perfectly.

"Turn left heading 280, turn right heading 040. Descend and maintain two thousand. Climb and maintain four thousand."

My voice smoothly flows through the intercom, utilizing all my "sadistic tendencies" to the maximum. With the corner of my eye, I see that John starts sweating profusely. His grip on the yoke becomes firm and stiff.

★ ★ ★

Let's press the Pause button now. What are my options at this time?

I could ask John, "Are you feeling OK?"

But I know that he, as I too would do, will go straight into the DENIAL defense mechanism and keep pushing forward. Our egos do not allow us to admit to such a thing. Since I would rather go home after this flight than spend time cleaning the aircraft, it does not look like an attractive option.

I could stop the lesson, but then he will probably say something AGGRESSIVE like, "Why? We haven't finished everything we talked about. How about recoveries from the unusual attitudes you presented on the ground?"

I could ask him why he is holding the yoke so firmly and ask him to loosen the grip, but then John would probably RATIONALIZE or PROJECT his response.

As you can see, I have not one but four potential defense mechanisms to disarm before they occur.

★ ★ ★

"John, why don't we look outside together for a moment. Can you tell me what that mountain in front of us on the horizon is? I think I went skiing there at some point. You know this turning and climbing is making me nauseous. It always does."

★ ★ ★

Let's press the Pause button.
What I am doing here are as follows:

- I recognize the impending problem.
- I provide the solution to the problem. The best way to mitigate nausea is to stabilize your senses by looking at the horizon.
- I give my student a way out. If I can get nauseous, then it is acceptable for him to get sick. He will not feel defeated or humiliated.
- The problem becomes nonexistent, and defense mechanisms are avoided.

Now we can press Play again.

★ ★ ★

As we try together to figure out the name of one of the mountains in New Hampshire, there is a visible "foam" forming out of cumulus clouds to our northwest. Thunderstorms were not forecast until later that night, but the way it looks, I know they will be all over the area within an hour. Also, air decided to start moving and create a little shiver of turbulence. It is time to head back home.

We turn in the direction of the airport. The sports stadium in Attleboro provides us with an excellent first visual point before we will be able to see the airport. It is also a good reporting point when you call Norwood Tower. I don't need to tell John what to do. He flips frequency on one of the radios, and together we listen to the current ATIS (automatic terminal information service). With its two 4,000 foot runways heading north-south and east-west, Norwood can accommodate any winds most of the time. We discover that runway 35 is in use with a significant variable left crosswind. Of course, we could ask for another runway, but the wind has decided to create a crosswind regardless of what runway we will use.

In the meantime, I must have done something to upset the weather gods. The airplane is being tossed up and down and side to side. The wind seems to be enjoying itself at our expense and having some fun with us. It is far from being dangerous, but it stopped being pleasant some time ago. The dilemma crossing my mind is if I should take control and land or allow John to have his first significant crosswind component landing. I decide on the second option. Let's be adventurous.

We contact the tower, which is instructing us to report 3 miles left base to runway 35. Besides us talking to the controller, there is a silence on the frequency. Most likely, and smartly so, everybody else I know is already drinking cold beer, planting their feet firmly on solid ground. We report base to the tower, and we are cleared to land. The airplane is now behaving like a newly saddled wild horse trying to remove its potential owner from its back. I rest my hand on the dashboard in a way it can quickly travel to take over controls if needed as we discuss variable crosswind technique.

John is not a stranger to crosswind landings. It's just this incredible fury of gusts he is being introduced to today.

"It is going to take a lot of work to land today. Just do what you know is necessary. You know how to do it. Just do your best. If we will not land perfectly on the centerline today, it is perfectly fine. I will take controls if, at any point, I determine that you need help. And there is nothing wrong with that at your stage of the training."

Like a tamed mustang, the airplane is touching the concrete with its left leg first to put the rest of its three hooves on the ground just a second later.

As we taxi off the runway with the left turn, small droplets of rain start showing up on the windshield. Once more, I will be able to go home to celebrate my "miraculous survival."

★ ★ ★

As an exercise, I will let you, this time, figure out on your own what potential defense mechanisms I was able to disarm in this last scenario.

CHAPTER

8

Going Back to Basics and The True Building Blocks

One early summer, like many times before, I took my wife and our grandson to a local farm for fruit picking. As with every year, we started with strawberries—nice, red, impressive, hanging low above the ground, looking ripe and delicious. And then the reality kicked in. After just one bite, I noticed a total absence of any real strawberry taste or smell. We promptly moved to a field full of blubbery bushes. The impressiveness was there too. Dark berries, the size of a small cherry, were inviting all guests to the area. Trying one of those, to my horror, I realized that they taste almost the same as our previous pick. Grapes gave me the same experience.

Do you remember how real strawberries, blueberries, or grapes taste and smell? If you are my age, you probably do. I'll never forget the outer wall of my grandmother's house in Warsaw, Poland, covered with grapes with its distinctive wine-like aroma and flavor; or the basket of blueberries that would make your hands blue upon touching and their unmistakable taste. How have we managed to produce different fruits that look so nice but taste the same?

I am sure by now you are probably asking, What in the world, Radek? Does this have anything to do with aviation? It does, and let me explain why.

In recent years, walking around air shows like AirVenture, Sun 'n Fun, and others or reading aviation magazines, I have noticed one strange thing. Modern aircraft avionics, autopilots, PFDs (primary flight displays), and MFDs (multifunction displays) spring to life all around us. We have ForeFlights, Garmins, and others. But I have a strong feeling that just like the fruit I was talking about, they all "taste" the same. They all give us the same overload of information, served using slightly different knobs and buttons. I am finding it harder to get excited by one in the cockpit screen versus any other.

Please don't take me wrong. Those of you who know me for a long time will tell you that I was always an aviation and technology geek. Although I could not still afford it all, I always wanted to have the latest and most modern gadgets available on the market. But there is one aspect of it that is now disappearing very quickly: they were all different. For example, a Garmin 430 versus a KLN 94 GPS each had an entirely different "flavor." Do you remember those? Also, all the technology developed at that time was to support and assist our basic flying skills. You still had to input and interpret the data available on sometimes a very simple screen with just a digital CDI (course deviation indicator) or some numbers. Walking around airports and looking into cockpits of different airplanes or flying them with my students would always give me those days a different experience and flavor of aviation.

In both the Air France 2009 deadly crash and the Colgan Air Flight 3407 near Buffalo, investigators concluded that automation's dependence is eroding a pilot's basic flying skills. In my opinion, we are missing the point. More often now than ever, we never learn the "basic flying skills" in the first place.

Most flight school owners and managers insist on marketing and making available the newest and the greatest to their new students. Somehow, I can't imagine a student pilot on their first solo cross-country looking out the window rather than watching the magenta line if it is available to them. And yet situational awareness is the one and most crucial skill critical not only in visual conditions but also in the instrument environment. Then there is the feeling of the aerodynamics, speed, pitch, etc. Getting lost on a one-hour flight with five hours of fuel can benefit the student pilot more than following the magenta line correctly to their destination. I know. I got lost as a student pilot at least a few times.

We tend, these days, to try to find immediate solutions rather than look for the long-term objective. My prediction is that if we continue the current path in five to ten years, any loss of automation will be met with a total lack of skill that was never acquired in the first place.

In my opinion, the solution is very straightforward, but we need to implement it right away to result in positive outcomes years in the future. We must conduct all private pilot training on the most basic equipment. The same should apply to the instrument rating. Only then, after completing those, can we proceed to a different "high-tech" certification or endorsement as an advanced skill to learn and implement.

Teaching aviation is no different from any other area of education, whether formal or implemented by our lives' needs. Whether intended or by its course, any productive education, if it will result in an intended outcome, is done by the process of building blocks. We are not inventing anything new. The old saying "You have to crawl before you walk" is timeless and unmistakably real, from learning how to turn on the lights in a room through basic activities in life to aviation. The system and chain of principles are unquestionably the same. To build, we need the foundation of basics first. Then we need to have a set of elements with a full understanding of their applicability. And only then can we start putting everything together.

The most important thing before we start is to be excited and passionate about what we do. Don't be afraid to be yourself; be unique and creative. Please do not go out and look for a successful personality to try to duplicate. Remember, creativity creates progress. Without being progressive throughout history, humankind would probably still be lighting candles and the Wright brothers would never have their first flight in 1903.

The so-called standardization that is wrongly understood so many times is hampering aviation education in so many flight schools in the world. As defined by *Merriam-Webster Dictionary*, *standardization* means "to bring into conformity with a standard especially in order to assure consistency and regularity." But standardization is also the process of creating procedures to guide the creation. Standardization is about policies and the outcome, also defined by dictionaries as "a level of quality or attainment," but it is never about the process itself. Be unique. Avoid a canned approach. Be one of those teachers who we remember years after graduation. Of course, you will need to follow your flight school's syllabus, and if they don't have it, create one of your own. It is easier than you think. But if you can find your more effective ways to explain lift or left-turning tendencies or teach landings, by all means, do it. But to go along with this chapter's primary subject, let's talk about a fundamental building block first—one individual flight lesson and its block elements.

FAA defines the building block concept as a learning concept that new knowledge and skills are best based on a solid foundation of previous experience or old learning. As knowledge and skills increase, the base expands, supporting further comprehension. I couldn't agree more.

All lessons should and will have many elements. But each should have only one measurable and primary objective— block. It should also have some previous blocks. Remember the Maslow's pyramid and the learning laws of primacy, intensity, and effect we talked about in the earlier chapters? Here is where they all come to play together. Here is where you will be creating those, as I call them, WOW effects. And each lesson has to have one to be effective. My standard lesson cycle (SLC) formula is straightforward (fig. 4), and I employ it in any situation I need to teach.

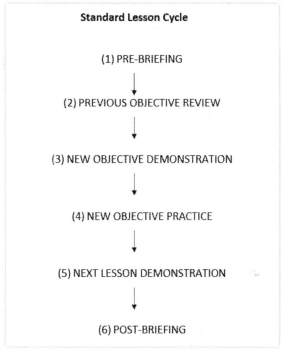

Figure 4

Let me elaborate. The core of the cycle itself is between steps 2 and 5. I can illustrate this as a real building structure (fig. 5).

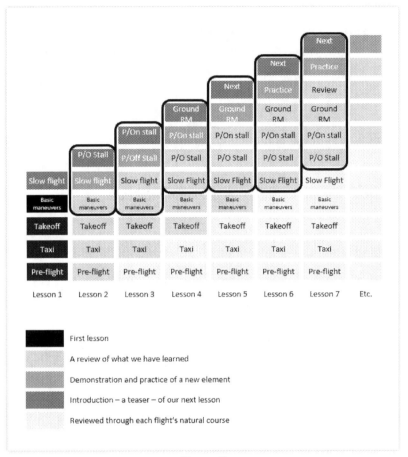

Figure 5

As you can see from this graph, each subsequent lesson will always have three elements (blocks) from the second lesson as we advance. They are a review of what we have learned (light gray), demonstration and practice of a new element (darker gray), and introduction—a teaser—of our next lesson (very dark grey). The number of blocks in the review step will grow with time. As you progress, the review blocks will start being reviewed through each flight's natural course (very light gray). How steep this line of "self-review exercise" will advance will depend on the progression of your student's abilities. I introduce landings after we practice slow flight and power-off stalls during the third lesson. From that point on, they become a permanent part of the review-exercise element, and that is why I am not showing them on the building block graph.

The entire cycle of each lesson should last for about two hours and thirty minutes. I am talking about the time from when a student is already in your office, and you say, "Today we are going to be learning about _____." Don't cut yourself short and do a disservice to your client by the so-called 0.3 pre plus post. Most of you know what I am talking about here. If a flight instructor charges their student for nine minutes of briefing and nine minutes debriefing, they either give their services for free or don't do their job. In any case, it is not professional behavior, and it makes it hard to measure any progress. We can't progress unless we have a quantifiable record of what we do. Your students will quickly realize that they "get what they paid for," and they will move along to a different flight school right away or when the time comes for their next rating. Any allocation lesser than two and a half hours will create an atmosphere of a rush. More time than that will make your student tired and unable to comprehend the material allocated for the lesson. Now let's take a look at each element of my formula individually.

SLC 1—Briefing. In step 1, we are laying down our lesson's objectives. Be precise. Ask probing questions to know your client better. If the answer to your question "What do you do for a living?" is "I am an aerodynamic engineer," you may adjust your ground lessons slightly. Know precisely what you want to accomplish during your flight. Show exact measurement factors. I always lower expectations as to the outcome, stating that I don't expect my student to be perfect on the first try, but we will work to get as close as possible to our final standard. It is worth mentioning here that FAA standards are grossly misunderstood by most of our general aviation industry. For example, the so-called plus or minus hundred feet on altitude hold is not a standard. It is an allowable deviation from the bar. The standard is assigned altitude.

If this is my first lesson after an intro flight, my first objective will always be preflight and taxiing. It is the time when I am going to get my student READY and excited. I will explain how it is done and the fact that I will be handling any flight elements we will not address during this session, including any radio communication. I will explain that they don't need to judge themselves about anything that is not the lesson's objective and may perform during this flight.

SLC 2—Previous objective review. If this is not our first lesson, there are some elements your student has learned during their previous sessions. This list will be growing with time, and you will be reviewing some parts through the natural course of the flight. For example, the RECENCY of a preflight, taxiing, takeoff, etc. will happen due to every flight's nature. Some other elements like slow flight or stalls will need to be addressed as you progress individually. I will walk you through a typical lesson of mine as an example in this book's next chapter. For now, let us move to the next element of our standard lesson cycle formula.

SLC 3 and 4—New objective demonstration and practice. In this activity, we will employ something well-known to us already. If you are a flight instructor, it was on your written test and oral quizzes. You may even have been asked about it during your CFI check ride. A demonstration-performance method. We use it to control mental or physical abilities that require practice, and the demonstration-performance method is based on the belief that people learn by performing. In this method, students observe the skill performed by an instructor and then try to replicate it themselves.

If it is my first lesson with this student, the new objective is accomplished on the ground and involves preflight and taxiing.

Here is when you can get creative to ensure that the PRIMACY and INTENSITY are satisfied and the EFFECT is pleasant and positive. You will EXERCISE this element over and over again, so the RECENCY should also be happy. "Radek, what do we do for the rest of this first lesson?" you may ask. That first lesson is always slightly different. As a beginning of a beautiful journey, we are just starting when there is nothing behind, yet everything is in front of us.

One maneuver that I "demonstrate" purely by explaining is the takeoff. The WOW factor was already accomplished during the intro flight. Now is the time for a "supervised performance." During that first lesson, we also go to the practice area, where after I show them how to change altitudes and make turns, they take controls and fly "wherever they want." There are no altitudes to hold and no standards to uphold. I utilize my ingenuity and imagination to make it as enjoyable as possible and implement the law of intensity as much as practical.

If it is not our first lesson, we will review and practice maneuvers we have learned so far and progress to what we briefed on the ground and what I introduced at the end of our last lesson.

SLC 5—Next lesson demonstration. It has one and only one purpose. Here is where all the laws of learning will accumulate, and Maslow's pyramid will demonstrate itself in its full majesty and glory. Up to this point, the entire flight should have been INTENSE (in the positive sense), with a positive EFFECT and PRIMACY satisfied. It should give your client the feeling of a positive accomplishment and an ability to make them READY to look forward to the next pleasant, satisfying event. In other words, when they go home, they will be able to "brag" not only about what they have learned today but also about what they will be doing next time. You want them to say, "I can't wait for our next lesson."

SLC 6—Debriefing. Debriefing should be honest and precise. Review the lesson with all its elements. Ask probing questions to get to know the client even better. "Was the airplane's behavior what you had expected?" Point out everything that they will be practicing to make it better with time. Make it positive. Catch them doing something right and point it out. Most likely, you will hear a lot of questions. You don't have to know EVERYTHING. None of us do. There is no reason to be artificial about it. If there is time, find that answer together. And remember, knowledge through understanding. "Why does an airplane descend when we reduce power?" If your student is an aerodynamics engineer, take advantage of it and do not be afraid to ask her or him to teach you even more. There is so much I have learned from my students along all these years.

CHAPTER

9

Maneuver as An Exercise

You have probably heard about scenario-based training (SBT). What is scenario-based training? According to the FAA website, *scenario-based training* is a training system that uses a highly structured script of real-world experiences to meet flight training objectives in an operational environment.

The SBT has been with us for some time now. Mostly misunderstood, in my opinion, by many flight schools and instructors, it can be an excellent tool in certain stages of the training. Implementing it from the very first lesson may be a big mistake. Have you ever taken dance lessons? I have, and they all start with a basic step first and no music. I am not a great dancer, and the law of recency plays a significant role in this equation. Therefore, once every few years, we usually take the dance course with my wife. It always starts the same way: "Leading person left foot first and walk." I can't imagine my dance instructor coming in, turning on music, showing very complicated tango moves, and asking us to repeat them. Somehow, it is how we tend to teach in aviation. Please don't overload your students with the cockpit environment's complexity, which may be easy and obvious for you, but not for them.

★ ★ ★

7B2 in Northampton, Massachusetts, was, is, and will always be my favorite airport. It's only 3,000-foot-long and 50-foot-wide runway 32-14 is bordering Highway 91 on the west side and Connecticut River on the east. The departure end of runway 14 is pointing directly at the Mount Holyoke mountain range. A small two-story building to the ramp's side is housing the FBO (fixed base operator) and our flight school. The launch area adjacent to the dispatch desk on the first floor always attracts local pilots and aviation enthusiasts. Many of them are my students or my friends or both. There are no fences or gates. Three Piper Warriors and a Cessna 172 are parked on the grass bordering the concrete ramp in front of the FBO.

The outside wooden staircase leads to the upper deck and an entrance to the classroom. My small office with a large wooden desk and window pointing to the road on the other side of the building is also up there.

If there is such a thing as an authentic flavor of general aviation, it is happening here. 7B2 opened as LaFleur Airport on April 1, 1929. Many historic aviators, including Charles Lindbergh, Ruth Nichols, and the Granville brothers, flew here. Today I am just a humble follower of the great aviators, with only my thoughts and dreams.

Northampton, Massachusetts—view from the deck to the southeast

The lounge chair on the deck is emitting a squeaky sound every time I move, as it would want to disturb my deep contemplation. It is early May, just past eight in the morning, and the air smells of freshly cut grass. Some lonely Piper is practicing landings in the airport's traffic pattern under the sky covered with a solid stratus cloud, as it would want to compete with a lawn mower noise finishing its work behind the hangar. I can feel the breeze as it is rising from its deep sleep at night. The forecast is calling for relatively high but steady winds from the south generated by a distant low pressure to our west.

"It is going to be a perfect day," I say out loud to myself.

My first student today is Sue, a young woman in her late twenties who wants to be a flight instructor. It is just her second lesson, but she is determined in her aviation dreams. As a child and then a teenager, she came to this airport to watch airplanes taking off and landing. Now she is back to fulfill her desire to become a professional aviator.

I look at my watch. The dial is mercilessly showing twenty-five past eight. Since our lesson is scheduled for eight thirty, it is time to go. I overcome the laziness of my body and stand up to walk downstairs. It would not be professional to be late. I pride myself on always being on time to the minute.

We review some basics from our previous discussions during our ground session involving preflight, takeoff, and basic maneuvers. Then I introduce Sue to the concept of a slow flight maneuver. It is going to be our first true "building block"—our first step in this aviation dance class. I explain how this maneuver is done and its intent. We will start developing, practicing, and mastering our skills to "feel" the airplane. It is us who will be flying, not the aircraft, which serves only as our extension. The machine merely allows us to be in the air. We are the masters of our destiny. We will also be learning today the relation between ground speed and airspeed.

"Oh, by the way! Have you ever flown an airplane backward?" I ask.

Her eyes light up.

"Really? Can it be done?" she says.

"With a little good luck and favorable winds, we may be doing it today," I add.

Preflight under my watchful eye goes as expected. Sue doesn't miss any items from her checklist. The fuel tanks of our Piper Warrior are almost full. I used only forty minutes of fuel this morning as I went for a practice flight myself earlier. As we taxi to the runway 14, just as I hoped, the wind sock is rising almost straight up and unmistakably is showing which runway to use. After a detailed run-up, when we check every available system that could fail, we make sure the final to runway 14 is empty. I push on the microphone switch and announce our departure.

The Piper is slowly moving along the hard surface of the runway. If it weren't for the wind sock pointing directly at my nose, I wouldn't know there is any wind at all today. It feels like the invisible hand is holding the aircraft back, but the airspeed indicator is already at its rotation speed. Simultaneously, some mysterious force pulls us from the ground on its own without any input on controls.

My right hand is resting on the dashboard to show my student that they are in control and I am not helping her. Of course, she doesn't know that hours of practice allowed me to figure out how to react within a split second if needed. The Mount Holyoke Range in front of us seems to be running to meet us head-on. The terrain becomes almost reachable from the cockpit. I know, of course, this is just a visual illusion. Sue knows that already too. As we are quickly gaining altitude, I announce again on the radio our northeast departure. We gently bank to the left to exit the traffic pattern via crosswind, perpendicular to the runway centerline.

The trip to the practice area, which is located in the vicinity of the University of Massachusetts in Amherst, and to the east of the Connecticut River takes just five minutes. The wind is on our tail. The tall building of the university's campus is pointing its finger at us in the sky above. I can see a reflection of the morning sun in the mirror-smooth surface of the reservoir to our east in the distance. To our left, a dark-blue ribbon of the Connecticut River is warming its body in the morning sun like a giant python. Now it is time to have some fun.

We start with what I call stretching exercises. Any good training session has to have good stretching exercises first. We begin with two clearing turns. With our first turn to the east, I can feel the wind pushing us to our practice area boundaries. We make another clearing turn, this time to the south. It crosses my mind that any turn downwind with this wind would take us on a cross-country flight.

First, I review what Sue learned in our previous lesson just a few days ago. I know how RECENCY and EXERCISE are essential to aviation training. But also today we are trying to capture specific assigned numbers. I am coming up with different altitudes and headings to intercept. Sue seems to have no problems following my instructions. After riding this self-inflicted roller coaster for what seems like an eternity but lasts for only ten minutes, I ask for controls.

"My controls!" I announce to her without any delay in my headset through the aircraft's intercom.

"Your controls!"

"My controls!" I promptly acknowledge.

Explaining verbally every single step I take, I reduce power to 1,500 rpm. Right away, I can feel this invisible force of gravity that wants to bring the aircraft to its chest. Back pressure on the yoke is preventing any loss of altitude. My right foot starts working gently on the rudder pedal. The airspeed indicator is moving steadily counterclockwise. Airspeed is now within the flap deployment speed. I reach down for the flap handle and deploy all three positions. Like someone who suddenly decided to stand up, the airplane is making its last attempt to climb slightly, but the simple ease of the back pressure on the yoke is preserving my objective. I look briefly at my altimeter.

The indicator's needle is glued to 3,000 feet and is not moving at all. From this point forward, it is going to be the only instrument I will use. The instructor has to be perfect. This brief thought crosses my mind. It is precisely why I was exercising this maneuver by myself this morning, as I have done so many times before. My eyes are moving between the outside world and altimeter reading. The altitude reading is not changing, but I can feel a little shiver of a buffet and the impending sink of just a few feet with my body. My hand gently moves the throttle to 2,100 rpm. I know those numbers by heart, and they are slightly different for each airplane. Like people, they all have their individual personalities. Slight trim adjustment relieves any pressure on my arm, but my right foot works much harder at this time. We fly right on the edge of a stall. Our stall warning indicator is chanting its song gently like a bird in the morning sun. We make a few shallow turns with wings, making almost no bank angle.

I didn't say too much about this, but purposely I maneuvered myself into the wind direction head-on. I know Sue is watching my every move in the cockpit without paying too much attention to the ground.

"Look down!" I say.

And then she notices for the first time. We are not moving. Our friendly Piper Warrior has suspended itself above the ground like in some impossible surrealistic dream.

"WOW!" I hear in my headset. "I didn't know it is possible!"

Now I know we have our planned INTENSE moment. Maybe we will have a chance to fly backward the next time. But it is still amazing.

It's time to EXERCISE. Without changing anything in the configuration, I keep guiding the airplane through the air.

"Your controls," I announce.

I always let my students experience the maneuver of a well-configured airplane first. Then I guide them through the recovery and full-entry procedure. We practice it over and over again with some mixed results but still a lot of fun.

It is now time to start thinking about heading home. I know with this wind, it will take a lot longer than our trip to the practice area.

"Have you ever thought what would happen if we entered a stall?" I ask her as we are practicing our slow flight for the last time today. "Let me show you. It is a perfectly safe maneuver at this altitude. We are going to learn and practice it during our next lesson. Today I am just going to demonstrate it. I am not going to be recovering from it right away on purpose to show you what to expect. My controls!"

As she hands control over to me, my left hand checks the carburetor heat handle that is already on throughout this entire maneuver anyway. I gently reduce the power to idle. Aft pressure on the yoke at first prevents any altitude loss, but then the stall warning buzzer starts crying a constant warning noise loudly. The buffet, to which we got used by now, is transferring itself in a gentle brake. The airplane's nose falls below the horizon. My firm grip is holding the yoke back as far as I can. My feet dance on the rudder pedals like on the dance floor to keep us coordinated. Like a dolphin in the ocean, the Warrior is bringing its nose up above the horizon. Then it gives in and dives below again. Falling like a leaf, I let the airplane sink for about 1,000 feet. Then I bring it back to a regular level flight with a standard gentle nose down, one notch of flaps up, and power on recovery.

We will be coming back to master and EXERCISE this maneuver many more times over and over again. Now it is time to return to the airport.

"Your controls!"

★ ★ ★

Think hard before exposing your student to the full and complicated one-hour-long choreography of the entire "tango," using an ill-understood and wrongly advised scenario. And before they fully master, appreciate and understand their basic steps.

We can still have fun and an enormous sense of accomplishment by using maneuvers. And then they have to become our routinely performed exercise.

CHAPTER

10

Teaching Cross-Country

Situational Awareness

Jack, or Jacek, as he wants us to call him, is one of our students from Poland. He is a pragmatic thinker rather than an abstract or philosophical one. In general, pilots tend to be logically oriented. He has a small figure, short stature, and dreamy eyes, which conflict with his character. Or maybe we, pilots, are all "analytical dreamers" or "dreamy analysts."

Jacek arrived from Poland four weeks ago in April, and he is already a student pilot with the local solo flight endorsement he received from me last week. I have to say the weather has been cooperating for him so far. We were able to practice various wind and weather conditions, and not a single day kept us on the terra firma. He plans to get his pilot training here in the USA and go back to Poland to convert it to a European one. From what I am hearing from most of my international students, it is much less expensive to do it this way. His ultimate dream is to fly for the LOT Polish Airline.

I always try to schedule my beginner cross-country students in the morning to avoid any extra distractions like turbulence or thunderstorm building in the afternoon. I know there is still a little chance of any of those events happening in early May, but still, you never know.

My philosophy is always traveling to the west on those flights, not only because we have an ocean to the east. It is also because most of the cold fronts in this part of the world come from the northwest and west. Travel in that direction allows us to encounter any weather head-on and the ability to turn back and escape to our home airport if we need.

It is going to be Jacek's first dual lesson with me after his few local solo flights. I have already told him yesterday we will start going to other airports. He wanted to know right away if he should try to prepare any flight plans or dead-reckoning calculations. I knew he was studying hard all that material, but I just smile mysteriously and say, "You will not need any of that."

His eyebrows raise for a moment as he would want to say, "What do you have in mind?"

No, I am not thinking about GPS, even though we have those in our airplanes now. I have something entirely different on my mind.

Today he is going to discover, I think, smiling to myself.

I am always at the airport way ahead of my students and, in many cases, my flight instructors or even the office staff. As a chief flight instructor, I want to make sure that everything is the way we left it last night and airplanes are fueled and ready to go. I also get a full weather briefing for local flights and any potential destinations. I want to be able to question somebody's judgment during the day if necessary. I have not done it yet, and I doubt I will ever do it, but I always remember that "swiss cheese" safety model. And I want to be safe. The more layers, the better. Of course, I wouldn't let any of them know I do that. I don't want to create any appearance that I don't trust my crew. I value them too much.

Norwood flight school's crew (2008) with
the author *(second from the right)*

I supervise two locations for this sizable flight school in the northeast, one here in Norwood and the other in Providence, Rhode Island. At both locations, I would put my life in the hands of any of those who work with me. I am building not only excellent work relations but also friendships that will last for years to come. They are my dream team.

Jacek walks in through the door exactly as scheduled at eight in the morning. We exchange some greetings in Polish but then quickly switch to English. Even though English is my second language, it is my primary when it comes to aviation. Maybe it is just my laziness. It feels like it would be challenging for me to find translations and definitions in my native language when I have learned the entire professional vocabulary in another language. Jacek's English is fluent anyway, and he needs to communicate in it for his tests and check rides regardless.

"So what are we going to be doing today?" he asks.

"We will try to find Northampton Airport about 65 miles to the west," I say.

"But I didn't prepare any nav logs," Jacek responds.

"Pilotage, my friend, pilotage!" I reply and start explaining what we will be doing.

My plan is always straightforward, and my objective is clear. I want my students to fly knowing where they are by seeing the world around them. I want them to experience aviation as it was at its very beginnings. I want them to treat any additional instrumentation like a VOR, ADF, or GPS as supporting equipment only—equipment allowing them to conduct those flights with more precision but not using them as their primary source of VFR (visual flight rules) navigation. This lesson is also my PRIMARY introduction to my students of the importance of situational awareness in flight. I want them to develop that type of attention, which let Captain Sullenberger, in an emergency, ditch a US Airways Airbus A320 on the Hudson River on January 15, 2009.

Like in any other training phase, in cross-country instruction, I also use true building blocks by adding new elements as we are introduced to the basic blocks first. You will not find those lessons designed the way I do it in any commercially designed syllabus. It is my system that I developed. It takes a few extra steps, but it will benefit students for a lifetime of flying.

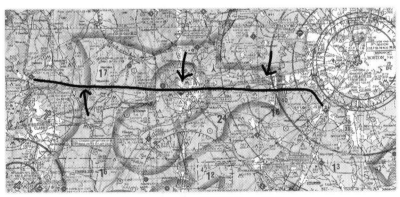

Cross-country KOWD to 7B2

"Here is how we are going to do it, Jacek," I start explaining, drawing a map on the sectional with my finger. "Today we will take off on the runway heading north. After the launch, we will see in the distance an ocean to our right. It means east, as you can see here on the map. We will turn left to leave the ocean behind us. The destination is to the west of us. What is the first sizable town you will see? Framingham. If we don't see it, there is the next one you should see clearly— Worcester." I put my finger on the yellow shape on the paper next to the small blue circle identifying a tower-controlled airport. "We will point ourselves there and fly over it."

As I explain following waypoints, Jacek is nodding with understanding. I should add to him that the view out of the cockpit may be slightly different from what we see on the sectional, but I want him to discover it himself. Let's make it INTENSIVE.

Of course, at this stage, it is the student's decision if they want to fly. I will only stop them if it is not safe. If the student's determination is not to fly in some marginal situation, I will respect their decision even though I can determine it is safe. They need to learn their pilot in command (PIC) responsibility, and they need to see that others will respect their judgment.

Jacek is calling Flight Service to obtain his weather briefing. Of course, I act as if I know nothing about the weather this morning. I stay near the phone with him if he needs any help, but help is not necessary this time. He hangs up and explains the situation. Prevailing winds are out of the north, there are some scattered clouds at 7,000 feet, and visibility is more than 10 miles. This forecast is holding at least until noon, when we can expect a slow cold front to visit us from the northwest. But since the temperature is around seventy degrees, we should not expect any violent weather to develop anyway.

"What do you think?" I ask.

"Lecimy!" Jacek replies in Polish, which means "We are going flying."

We grab our flight bags and headsets and head out to the ramp. I already have the airplane keys and clipboard with times with me.

He follows the checklist religiously as he walks around this fifteen-year-old Cessna 172. It is Jacek's responsibility to do the preflight. But if anything goes wrong, we will both die on the same airplane. Regardless of how much I can sacrifice for my students, I still plan to live a long and happy life. So I pretend that I don't pay any attention, but I see his every move and check. On occasion, out of "curiosity," I ask "How much fuel do we have?" or "How much oil is left in the engine?"

Jacek is done with his preflight.

"How do we look?" My question sounds very formal, but I already know what the answer is.

Jacek already knows how to handle radio communications, but I offer to do it to avoid any additional distractions. Before we call ground control, we listen to the weather on the ATIS frequency. To my surprise, winds on the surface are calm. We get clearance to taxi to runway 35, and after a run-up, which we do just short of the hold-short line of the runway, we brief our emergency departure procedure. There are not many options in an emergency when you depart this runway, but I like to be prepared for all possibilities. What if we lose the engine while we are still rolling? What if it happens after takeoff and there is still runway remaining in front of us? What if it's not...? And so forth.

I switch frequency to the tower.

"Norwood Tower, Niner-Niner-Zero-Five-Foxtrot, ready at three-five, west departure," I say to my headset's microphone. I am not surprised that the same voice as we heard on the ground frequency is responding. Many times, the same person here in the tower will handle both functions.

"Zero-Five-Foxtrot, cleared for takeoff. Left turn approved."

The airplane is moving forward, gaining more and more speed. Jacek is verbally announcing as I like doing it.

"Airspeed alive, thirty, forty, fifty, rotation speed!" Then, "Positive rate of climb! No runway remaining!"

Now I am looking for the best place to land on the golf course ahead, just in case. I rehearse in my mind what I would say to the tower if we have an engine failure at this point. I always do it. Just a little obsession of mine. But so far, so good. Now we are at 800 feet, and I feel safe here. I look to the right and point out the ocean in the distance. Jacek knows what that means. He puts our Cessna in a left bank, and we start turning as we continue to climb. We need to remain below 4,000 feet here to get from under Boston's Bravo airspace. I switch the radio to Boston Approach just to listen and have it available if we need any help.

"So where are we going now?" I ask Jacek.

I see some confusion and concern on his face. I have seen that look on many of my students' faces in this exercise. Under us, we see sort of an anthill with streets and roads riddled in some giant puzzle someone is trying unsuccessfully to put together. But this is all about the big picture.

"Where is the ocean? Behind us. What is in front of us? Not what is under us!" I say.

Suddenly, the entire picture starts making sense. There is a distinct and well-visible city in the distance. Looking at the sectional, it has to be Worcester. Besides, there is a well-visible highway going straight through it. As Jacek's eyes follow the road in our direction, his face brightens with a smile.

"Lake on both sides of the highway and a small town—FRAMINGHAM!—to our right," he announces with almost silly enthusiasm, and he is right. We can follow that highway straight to Worcester, but there is no point in it. We can point the aircraft's nose there and travel directly to it. There is a definite right crosswind from the north, which is trying to push us south. We need to correct just enough for our ground track to be leading to our next waypoint.

"Where is the end of the Bravo airspace?" I pose a rhetorical-like question almost to myself. But Jacek has spent enough time with me already to know what that means. He adds power to start the climb to 4,500 feet. In Jacek's pre-solo stage, we spent all our time at or below 3,000. It is his first time getting to a higher altitude. As we settle comfortably at our cruise altitude, we are almost directly over the Worcester airport. I am still listening to Boston Approach, but I also have Worcester Tower on my other radio. Now we are eavesdropping on both frequencies.

At this altitude, the world opens itself with a different perspective. The higher we climb, the bigger the picture that we can see, comprehend, and appreciate. And this lesson is all about the big picture.

"So where is the ocean?" I ask again. Jacek is pointing in the right direction.

"What are we over?" is my next question. This time, I get another answer without hesitation.

"Worcester!" I hear in my headset.

"What is our next waypoint?" I keep investigating.

His eyes are scanning the horizon, where the large body of water makes itself well visible. After looking at the sectional, we both determine there is no other water body of that size around as we see on the map. It has to be the Quabbin Reservoir. All we have to do now is travel to its southern tip.

"Should we go to the left side of the reservoir?" I suggest and get immediate agreement to do so.

Finding 7B2 is not easy even for pilots flying out of there. I know, I was one of them. But on today's flight, water is our friend. *Thank God I don't have to fly over a desert,* I think to myself as we pass over the south end of Quabbin.

We are not going to be descending to the traffic altitude today. And we will not land there. The objective here is to find our last waypoint—our destination. Looking at the sectional chart together, we determine that the airport is just to the side of the U-shaped bend in the river, which is well visible from here.

At this time, I have two other frequencies on the radio: Bradley Approach and Northampton UNICOM. As we fly over

7B2 at 4,500, I want to call UNICOM to say a quick hello to some of my friends there. That is, of course, if there is a silence on the frequency, and there is.

"Northampton UNICOM, Zero-Five-Foxtrot!" In response, I get silence. They must be doing something outside or are busy with a client.

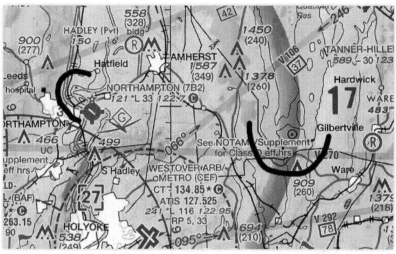

The U-shaped river and the southern edge of the Quabbin Reservoir

We turn back and climb to 5,500 feet. As we go over the Quabbin Reservoir's southern tip, I ask the same string of questions: where we are and what is next. But this time, from this altitude, we can see the city of Boston and the ocean right on the horizon. The only thing my student has to do is travel to the destination slightly right (south) of the city itself. As we get closer, the same landmarks will resurface again: highway with lakes on both sides to the left and the Norwood airport well visible straight ahead of us. No calculation, no nav logs with wind correction estimates, no dead reckoning with time checks. They all are going to be at our next lesson. For now, it is the first and fundamental block of any VFR flying—pure pilotage!

CHAPTER

11

Risk Management

Aviation does not have to be dangerous.

Let's discuss risk management. Risk management is about preparing and carrying out decisions that will minimize an activity's adverse effects. In our case, the potential adverse effects of a flight. The unfavorable effects of risk can be unbiased and measurable, like substantial damage to an airplane or property on the ground. Or it can be a significant impairment of a pilot or passengers or even loss of life. Or it can be subjective and difficult to calculate, such as damage to reputation due to a loss of your pilot certificate. By focusing on aviation risks and committing the necessary resources to control and mitigate risk, we protect ourselves from uncertainty. As I previously stated, general aviation flying is risky, but it does not have to be dangerous because of the available risk management.

Nobody ever taught me about risk management, from the private pilot certificate to a college diploma for my entire aviation education process. And yet almost every one of my teachers was talking about it. We did perform many elements of it by checking the weather or doing our exhaustive preflights. As a flight instructor, I continued the process of ignorance.

I emphasized to my students the importance of it without providing them with any concrete description or explanation. From what I have seen for decades, most general aviation pilots will intuitively conduct flight risk management assessments without any substantial scientific understanding of the process. It wasn't until later in my career that after getting some certificates in project and risk management and teaching college classes on the subject, I started fully understanding the process.

Let's start by stating that all aviation accidents and incidents are caused by human error, inability, or a particular decision. I can already hear some of you saying, "But, Radek, how about a catastrophic mechanical failure?" Very well, let's look at this example. The options here are the following:

- That particular part failed because of an inadequate preflight check—human error.

If not,

- That part failed because of its manufacturing—human error.

If not,

- That part failed because of its design—still human error.

If we get struck by lightning, it is still because of our inability to predict or avoid a thunderstorm. If the machine we fly is made by humans and flown by humans, the chain of causation will always point to us.

Once the risk and its source are identified, we can address it in a few different ways. Some of them, in some cases, may not necessarily be acceptable for us. But they are all valid.

A risk can be

- ignored,
- avoided,
- accepted,
- mitigated, and
- eliminated.

In the first case, we know the risk exists, and we still proceed forward. We IGNORE it. It may be proper if the event's likelihood is so low that the risk is unlikely to occur.

In the second point, we AVOID the activity entirely to avert the risk altogether. Let's say there is a forecast for heavy thunderstorms in the area. We don't fly.

In the third case, we know about the risk, but its severity is so low that we are willing to ACCEPT it. For example, our risk will be landing at an airport other than our intended destination.

And the fourth one is to MITIGATE. *Mitigate* is defined by *Merriam-Webster Dictionary* as "to cause to become less harsh or hostile." We mitigate, which means we lower any potential occurrence of a negative outcome. We mitigate any possible mechanical failure in flight by doing a preflight. We MITIGATE forgetting something in the process by using checklists. We mitigate by planning and coming up with plans B and C.

We can also ELIMINATE risk. For example, removing equipment that can overheat and start a fire will eliminate the fire's risk.

I promised this book not to be a textbook style, but I can't help myself to not suggest that you look over the risk matrix (fig. 6) form used by professionals. I am not implying you would do one before every flight. Just try it once to understand the process better, only as an exercise. Remember, understanding is the foundation of all knowledge.

Risk probability	Risk severity				
	Catastrophic A	Hazardous B	Major C	Minor D	Negligible E
Frequent 5	5A	5B	5C	5D	5E
Occasional 4	4A	4B	4C	4D	4E
Remote 3	3A	3B	3C	3D	3E
Improbable 2	2A	2B	2C	2D	2E
Extremely improbable 1	1A	1B	1C	1D	1E

Figure 6

Of course, you can make your colors and your scale as you wish.

The risk mitigation process will not be complete without mentioning the swiss cheese model. Imagine that one of those adverse and unpleasant events will move from one place of nonexistence to the other where it will show its ugly face. Now suppose that you are trying to stop it with a single slice of swiss cheese. When you bring the piece up to the light and look at it, you will see the light coming through the holes. If you put another slice of cheese on the first one, the chances are that fewer holes will line up with each other. The more pieces of cheese you have, the better the possibility that you will not see the other side. Those slices are just like our checklists, preflights, and all other layers of safety protection. The more layers you have, the lower is the possibility that something may slip through.

CHAPTER

12

Now is The Time for A Syllabus

A syllabus is a document that conveys material on the subject of a specific course of action and describes expectations and tasks. An aviation syllabus may be designed by a flight school, produced by a vendor (ASA, Jeppesen, etc.), or prepared by you, the teacher, who controls the course.

Just as it is impossible to perform any action in life without at least some basic plan, you will never be able to monitor progress in aviation without a syllabus. Some of you may say, "But, Radek, we have done our flying without any formal syllabus, and we are fine." The thing is that you did have a syllabus without even realizing that you did. Not all programs will be standard and formalized. For example, if I am going to make myself a cup of coffee, my syllabus will be to stand up, go to the kitchen, take coffee out of the cabinet, etc. You get the picture. Of course, I am not going to formalize it or put it on paper.

On the other hand, I would be doing a big disservice to my students if I wouldn't have a carefully designed plan for something as complex as aviation training. Yes, it can be done, but it will be chaotic and scattered. And it will take a much longer time and more money than necessary.

Even a commercially designed syllabus has to be understood and used correctly. Over the years, I have seen countless examples of misunderstood intent of how an aviation syllabus should be used. I have also seen a total misapplication of it in a flight school environment. The aviation syllabus is not a project plan where we check off completed elements and progress forward. It is a carefully designed map of building blocks positioned in a logical sequence. And the supporting blocks have to be revisited and reinforced regularly as we build and climb this training pyramid.

Most of those plans (syllabi) will consist of phases (stages) positioned in a logical structure. Progression to each next stage will be dependent on the completion of the previous ones.

Of course, we can try to complicate the entire issue here and take apart individual plan elements. The idea of this book is not to recycle any textbook knowledge. It is to help you understand the philosophy and intent of the entire process.

You can break down any private pilot syllabus into three stages.

- Stage I—Pre-solo (the first solo)
- Stage II—Dual cross-country flights
- Stage III—Solo cross-country flights

Of course, those are the main objectives, general goals, of each stage. They will be blended in with review lessons and student solo practice. Each class will have its particular purpose and elements. But their overall aim will always be there. Even in the 14 CFR Part 141 registered school environment, where training is strictly structured, you can apply your logical building blocks sequence and extend the time as needed as long as you cover all elements listed in the particular stage.

I like to give my own names to the above list of stages.

- Stage I—Let's have some fun (learning to walk).
- Stage II—Let's start going to other places.
- Stage III—You will be doing it all yourself (having fun on your own).

Before you start checking boxes on a list of items for one of the lessons from your school's syllabus, think first. What is the overall objective of the stage? And then start building with blocks in a logical sequence.

CONCLUSION

Whether you found it exciting or your curiosity took you on the trip, I am happy you are still here with me. Before you close the back cover of this book and put it away on a shelf or in some other form of storage where it will start gathering dust, please stay here with me a little longer. In this concluding chapter, I want to look at the bigger picture and see if I am just a lone wolf howling on an aviation landscape desert or if there is some dash of hope to make a change.

I wrote about this issue years ago, but my hopes, unfortunately, did not materialize. That is why I decided to write about it once more in this book. Sometimes persistence is what is needed.

I covered in this book a large part of my philosophy about the flight instructor approach that I think is appropriate for our mutual success. I wrote about my thoughts and feelings, and I took you along, my reader, on a few of my journeys. I hope you were there with me during those flights and I was able to pass along my thoughts and some of my dreams. I did present myself to you as a student pilot, pilot, and then a flight instructor. Although you can read this book in a few hours, it took me almost two decades to develop my flight instructor experience.

We can measure success in many ways, but when we try to address general aviation issues via meetings and conferences only, I confess to having mixed feelings about what is being accomplished.

I want to express a sincere thank you to all the organizers, volunteers, and organizations of all the safety and proficiency programs. By any measure, making those events happen is an impressive accomplishment and a giant step in the right direction. It also initiates a long-overdue discussion, but in my opinion, it is addressing a tiny segment of the pilot population.

Statistics from an industry study still show many new pilots dropping from their flight training. It, together with a low quality of education, is a cause for concern. In my belief, they call for a "full-blown alarm" and a "declaration of an emergency."

We cannot focus consistently only on short-term solutions. If we address all the problems now, we will see positive results in the future.

The question, however, is, *do all the meetings and programs accomplish what is needed?*

Some people who are overwhelmed by the euphoria of moving in the right direction, and the success of the single event or program itself may consider what I am about to say as some aviation heresy. But I hope they will understand that any progress and productive outcomes in history have always been characterized by vigorous debate. Let's have that debate.

One could say that first, we have to identify the problem, and only then can we look for a solution. But what is the real problem? There is no argument that many possible causes for GA training problems were already clearly identified by many of us. But in my opinion, the core of general aviation's sickness lies much deeper than we are willing to admit.

The problem is that our system of developing young professional pilots forces them to do something many of them aren't interested in doing—being instructors. To accomplish their goals, they have to "suffer" until their "time-building sentence" is over.

It has resulted in a large group of instructors who don't want to teach. But they are being put in that position by a flawed system through no fault of their own. No release or change of syllabus will make flight instructors use it properly. No FAA Advisory Circular or transition to Airman Certification Standards will create professionalism among them, especially among those who have no desire to be aviation educators.

But as long as the system requires young pilots to build hours by becoming CFIs, and it seems like it will be that way for a while, there are distinct steps we can take to make that system more effective. No one can or should change a young person's desires and dreams. But we can shape their behavior and attitudes through better supervision, coaching, and mentoring. And it can also be done by a student/client who needs to know what to expect and demand from their teachers. And I strongly hope this book does serve this purpose.

Short-term fixes may relieve us of short-term symptoms. Only long-term solutions based on an assessment of the big picture, in my opinion, make any sense. It will not yield immediate results, but the real fix lies in the outcomes that may show up in five or even ten years in the future.

There is only one way that we can accomplish this objective. We need to institutionalize the role of a career instructor. In the words of the former FAA administrator Randy Babbitt at the Pilot Training Reform Symposium in 2011:

> We can make rules to require certain professional behavior, but professionalism is a lot more than rule-driven behaviors. It's a mindset. It's an attitude that drives you to do the right thing— every time, all the time.

Creating a group of career instructors that will be available for years to come is our only salvation, and you can be one of them. Our long-term future is in our hands and does not require any regulatory change. It is up to us to guide, mentor, and demand a higher standard.

INDEX

M

N

O

P

Q

R

S

T

U

ABOUT THE AUTHOR

Born in Poland in 1960, Radek Wyrzykowski came to the US as a political refugee. As he attended the higher school of education in Rzeszow (Poland), he became involved in the student independence movement. When the Polish government declared martial law in December 1981, Wyrzykowski was imprisoned in January 1982. He came to the US in 1983. In January 2020, he was awarded by the Polish president the Cross of Freedom and Solidarity (Krzyż Wolności i Solidarności) for his activities to benefit a free and democratic Poland.

Radek obtained his professional pilot degree from Mohawk Valley, under the SUNY Albany program, and has more than six thousand hours dual given. He was a chief flight instructor for Horizon Aviation Inc. from 2007 to 2009 and a chief flight instructor for Northampton Aeronautics from 2005 to 2007. He was a correspondent and contributor to a Polish general aviation magazine, *PILOT Club*, where he published many of his articles. He is a certified flight instructor and instrument and multiengine instructor. He is the founder of IMC Club International and served as the president of that organization until 2015, when the program was acquired by the Experimental Aircraft Association (EAA). He serves now as a manager of Flight Proficiency at the EAA.

Radek may be reached through:

https://twitter.com/radek_imc
https://www.facebook.com/radek.cfi

Also by Radek Wyrzykowski

In this DVD/lecture presentation, Radek breaks down complex concepts in simple terms you can understand without a degree in meteorology.

Weather 101

"Uneven heating of the earth." What does it mean?

As the weather and climate change, it is a great time to focus on how it affects our flying. To that end, Radek presents *Weather 101*. What you will learn, you will be able to apply for practical purposes in your aviation activities.

Printed in the United States
by Baker & Taylor Publisher Services